DIVINE RELATIONSHIPS

DIVINE
RELATIONSHIPS

*Orchestrated by God
to Bless Your Life!*

RALPH F. DAWKINS

*D.Min. Senior Pastor,
Christian House of Prayer-San Angelo*

XULON PRESS

Xulon Press
2301 Lucien Way #415
Maitland, FL 32751
407.339.4217
www.xulonpress.com

© 2020 by Ralph F. Dawkins

Unless otherwise indicated, Scripture quotations taken from the
King James Version (KJV) – *public domain.*

Printed in the United States of America.

ISBN-13: 978-1-6305-0703-9

"And I will give them a heart to know me, that I am the LORD: and they shall be my people, and I will be their God: for they shall return unto me with their whole heart."
Jeremiah 24:7

To contact the author and publisher or to request permission to reproduce any parts or sections of this book, please contact:

Pastor Ralph Dawkins
Christian House of Prayer – San Angelo
333 West Avenue C, San Angelo, Texas 76903
325.653.0418

SPECIAL THANKS

———— ❋ ————

I would like to thank my Lord and Savior Jesus Christ for giving me such a profound revelation about the relationships the Father established around each of us to make our lives special. He is the air I breathe, the song I sing and I owe Him everything.

To my wife for life, Gwen, who has stayed with me these thirty-nine years through thick and thin. You are my best friend, my cherished companion and without you, this book would have no validity, for God has divinely blessed me to have you as my wife. I love You, BBG!

To my sons, Aaron (and Meghan) and Moshe (an Vanessa) and my precious grandchildren, Zoe, Judah, Ava and Mason who are another demonstration of what divine relationships is all about. Son Number 3, Mike T and the boys…I am honored to be your dad, and it is my desire to withhold no good thing from you.

To my sisters, Jean Harris and Rene Pulliam, and their families, thank you for your love and prayers and the spirit of family you have poured into me, even when time and distance didn't allow us to be together as often as we would have liked. Love you later, Love you lots!

To two of my Brooklyn brothers, Cal (and Dorena) Jones and Tim (and Joan) Rogers…Your friendship to me since we were teenagers is forever in my heart.

To my covenant brothers, Pastors Fred Moore, Austin, Texas, Anthony McCoy, Killeen, Texas, Darryl Simmons,

Tacoma, Washington and Drs. Jovaster Witcher, Waco, Texas and Derick Edley, Dallas Texas–your prayers, friendship and accountability are more precious than silver.

To the staff and precious membership of Christian House of Prayer–San Angelo, thank you for allowing me to shepherd you and for your support and encouragement. You make being a pastor a joy!

Lastly, To my bishop and his wife, the late Bishop Nathaniel and Valerie Holcomb of the Christian House of Prayer Ministries, Cathedral of Central Texas, Killeen, Texas for their love, guidance, and anointed example of what God meant when He said, "I will give you pastors after mine own heart" (Jeremiah 3:15).

TABLE OF CONTENTS

————— ❊ —————

FOREWORD

by Bishop Nate Holcomb

My favorite text in all the Bible is found in St. Matthew 16:13-19. Jesus was asking His disciples, *"Whom do men say that I the Son of man am?"* The disciples began with John the Baptist, Elijah, Jeremiah or just one of the prophets. Then, Jesus asked the disciples, *"Whom say ye that I am?"* Peter answered, *"The Christ, Son of the Living God."* Pastor Dawkins, through revelation from the Father and illumination of the Spirit, has captured the heart of the Lord as it relates to our relationship to the Godhead and consequently our relationship to one another.

The first of all the commandments Jesus quoted is, "... Hear, O Israel, the Lord our God is one Lord: And thou shalt love the Lord with all thy heart, And the second is namely this, Thou shalt love thy neighbor as thyself..." (Mark 12:29-31).

These two are the greatest commandments and both are the foundation for all true relationships. Pastor Dawkins' book on *"The Nature of Divine Relationships"* gives us God's laws, which are fixed principles, but also the pragmatics of the mind of Christ in how they are to be lived out in everyday life.

The old adage "No man is an Island" speaks to the very issue of relationship. No one can live successfully without understanding this important concept. "The Nature of Divine Relationships" is so impacting because it brings us back to the original maker and his design from the beginning. When something does not work right, we need to take it back to its maker. The Nature of Divine Relationships does just that, it brings us back to our Creator, and what he had in mind from the beginning.

Bishop Nate Holcomb Covenant Connections International Inc.

ACKNOWLEDGMENTS

———— ✳ ————

Divine Relationships, as given by the Holy Spirit to Pastor Ralph Dawkins is not just another literary work for reading. It is a revelation for living life daily which causes men to see the good works that comes from letting one's light shine that ultimately glorifies our Father in Heaven. The Holy Spirit, in this book, gives Pastor Ralph Dawkins heavenly principles for human practice and performance because of the importance of relationships to God. As you allow this revelation on relationships to regulate your living, The devil will be perpetually defeated, God will be powerfully exalted and Jesus Christ will be preeminent as Lord in and through your life.

Bishop Roderick Mitchell
New Life Church, Cleveland, Mississippi

In his book, *The Nature of Divine Relationships*, Pastor Ralph Dawkins, spiritually and practically provides a road map of understanding Divine Relationships rooted in the revelation of Sonship. The Phillips New Testament translation of Romans 8:19 says, "*the whole creation is on tiptoe to see the wonderful sight of the sons of God coming into their own.*"

What you will encounter in this timely book from Pastor Dawkins are practical principles and precepts that will provide you with understanding that, "*It was *always in His perfect plan to adopt us as His delightful children, through our union with Jesus, the Anointed One, so that his tremendous love that cascades over us would glorify His grace – for the same love He has for his Beloved One, Jesus, He has for us "*(Ephesians 1:5-6, The Passion Translation). We all need love, and we all need relationships, but our deepest needs for love and relationship can only be satisfied in the essential *Nature of Divine Relationships,* the wonderful sight of the sons of God coming into their own!

Dr. Gregory L. Cruell, Congregational Elder
Christian House of Prayer, Killeen, Texas

Congratulations Pastor Ralph, my friend on the latest edition of your book, *"The Nature of Divine Relationships."* WOW! What great content you have provided to the readers. You write from a perspective that is taken directly from the chapters of life that you have demonstrated toward those of us you call friend. This book will be a blessing and "go to" manual for those seeking friendships and relationships that are much more than just surface and superficial.

All the best,
Pastor Fred Moore
Kingdom of God Christian Center

INTRODUCTION

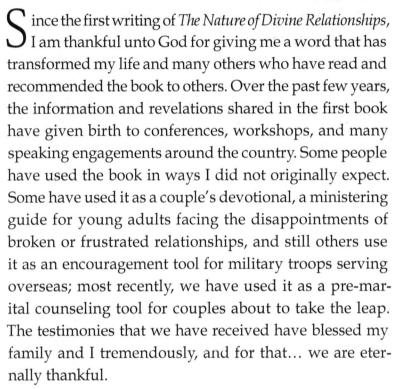

S ince the first writing of *The Nature of Divine Relationships*, I am thankful unto God for giving me a word that has transformed my life and many others who have read and recommended the book to others. Over the past few years, the information and revelations shared in the first book have given birth to conferences, workshops, and many speaking engagements around the country. Some people have used the book in ways I did not originally expect. Some have used it as a couple's devotional, a ministering guide for young adults facing the disappointments of broken or frustrated relationships, and still others use it as an encouragement tool for military troops serving overseas; most recently, we have used it as a pre-marital counseling tool for couples about to take the leap. The testimonies that we have received have blessed my family and I tremendously, and for that... we are eternally thankful.

This book, Volume II, will pick up where the last book left off. There are so many new insights I received that necessitated a second writing. This one however, is more of a literary journey and I pray that the insights you receive while reading this book will help you in cultivating healthy relationships wherever you go.

I never realized the impact this work would have on the lives of thousands of people who have read, re-read, and passed on this book to others needing clarity in their relationships.

For those of you who have not read the first book, I will introduce the subject matter by giving a quick review at the Nature of Divine Relationships and later what I will refer to as "Genesis Principles."

These principles are given to establish a point of reference during the creation processes that are present and active in our everyday lives. I pray that this book will be a blessing to you as it has been for so many others. I also pray that you will closely examine the relationships in and around your life as we journey through this book together. Enjoy!

A FRESH LOOK AT THE NATURE OF DIVINE RELATIONSHIPS

I received an e-mail from a friend a few years ago that said, "*People come into your life for 1) a reason, 2) a season, or 3) a lifetime.*" It is important to know and understand the differences.

When someone is in your life for a <u>reason</u>, it is usually to meet a need you have expressed outwardly or inwardly. They are there for the reason you need them to be. Then, without any necessary wrongdoing on your part or theirs, something happens that brings the relationship to an end. Sometimes they walk away, sometimes they move to another city, and sometimes they die. Either way, the reason or purpose of the relationship has been fulfilled, and you both move on. Years later, you may not remember their name or face, but once reminded of them, you can instantly go back to the details of your encounter.

When a person comes into your life for a <u>season</u>, it is because it is time for you or them to grow, share, or learn. When they come, they may bring you enlightenment and unique experiences that are invaluable for their future as well as yours.

Some seasons last longer than others, and as the season moves on, so will this unique person in your life. Should you encounter this person again, you will be able to remember some of the details without being reminded; you can recall the face or features of their character because you have shared some experiences together.

I read a snippet on Facebook recently that helped me understand seasonal relationships; it said,

There are some people in our life that we want to share our hopes and dreams with, simply because they've held that special place in our life before. In other words they were your "go to" person. But not everyone who was in your life is connected to where God is taking you. Everyone doesn't get to have access to your destiny. During your quiet time, God will reveal who is supposed to take the journey with you, and if it's not them, they need to quietly exit stage LEFT. This isn't personal, it's PURPOSE!

This statement could easily hurt the feelings of someone who may look at their inputs into another person's life as long term. But because destiny is a long-term dynamic, it shapes and calls us to people and places where God has prepared for us on the journey of life.

It is important to know that every relationship in your life right now is <u>not</u> a lifetime relationship.

<u>Lifetime</u> relationships teach lifetime lessons, which are things you must build upon in order to have a solid emotional and spiritual foundation. The ability to embrace these relationships is important to every person I know. Lifetime relationships don't need any assistance. They transcend family lines, years, states and are not limited to your last name. It is amazing how many details you can recall (names, dates, places, and faces) twenty or even thirty years later. Depending on the depth of your shared experiences, many relationships are transcendent and can be awakened when a reconnection takes place.

I recently connected with friends through social media that I haven't seen or spoken to in forty years. When we re-connected, it was as if time stood still, and because we had so many shared experiences, the details of the stories we exchanged was incredible! When we made contact, it started families linking up, which resulted in reunions, long overdue visits, and many hours of looking through photo albums and fond memories.

Social media can be a powerful tool in re-connecting with friends and relatives who you may not have seen in a long time, and I believe God can reconnect people together for a purpose that goes beyond their browsing.

A few things you need to know before we journey into this subject matter any further:

1. The truths regarding Divine Relationships are uni-versal. In other words, they work whether you are a Christian or not, they speak to every area of our lives, and like natural laws, they are ever present around us, whether we apply them or not.
2. Secondly, the concepts mentioned in this book can be applied to secular work relationships as well as those in the church and in your family.
3. Lastly, they are true in the natural as well as in the spiritual realm. In other words, they work harmoniously with other laws and principles.

Let the reader beware, however, after reading this book, you will begin to look more closely at the people and relationships around you, and you will be surprised at what you see.

As I began to search the Word of God for answers and insights to better understand the nature of divine relationships, a few key points jumped out me:

1. The Bible is a book about relationships. When God wanted to express how He would deal with mankind, He did so by way of relationships. You will see recurring terms like: "Father", "son", "family", "covenant", "heritage", "lineage", "adoption", and "generations", (and there are many more) laced from Genesis to Revelation about relationships.
2. Nearly every parable or story by Jesus was about relationships (including those about money).
3. The Father has a need that only we, as His children can fulfill. That's right! In all of His omnipotence, His omniscience, and His omnipresence, He has a need...and that need is to have His children reconciled to Him

The term "Divine" infers when God, the great maestro in the orchestra of life, brings people into and out of our lives, there is always a greater (divine) purpose behind who and where you are in life. When something is *Divine*, that means it is in the realm understood by religious people to be at the core of existence and has a transformative effect on their lives and destinies. It carries with it the connotation that God is involved or inspires it.

1. <u>Nature</u> is the material world, the essence of the natural world, as in mountains, trees, animals, or rivers.

2. A <u>Relationship</u> is defined as "the state and quality of being connected (i.e. Kinship or association).

So, the Dawkins Translation / definition of "Divine Relationships" is this…"an association or kinship inspired by God at the core of my existence that will have a transformational effect on my life and will shape my destiny."

Here's what the Lord showed me…Divine Relationships are orchestrated by God to bless your life!

Like a great composer and maestro of a symphony, our Heavenly Father knows the composition and what instruments should be played, when, how, and their timing, so that in the end, like a great concert performance, a great relationship will be created and everyone observing it will stand up and applaud you.

The Father knows when and how to bring people into your life to help you fulfill your *Life Assignment.* I have also discovered that there is a great deceiver who always tries to derail people by bringing counterfeit people who are only in your life to bring you down, discourage you, or take advantage of you.

This is a great deception, and it becomes vitality important to ask yourself the question, *"Why is this person in my life AT THIS TIME?"*

How many lives have been ruined because a certain person came in to a relationship, department, or even a church auxiliary and caused chaos, hurt, and harm? The deception, of course, is that things didn't start off that way! It never does!

Smooth talk, hype gear, new ride, and a favor for a favor can make a vulnerable person to drop their defenses to a wolf in sheep's clothing.

The point here is that every relationship is NOT divinely orchestrated. So, it is imperative to differentiate between those inspired by God from those that are not! Some relationships are created by our own strength, wisdom, or physical attraction and sometimes becomes our own tragedy or triumph. It is our own doing. So I am not speaking of the "Ishmael" type of relationships (Gen. 16), where Abraham, Hagar and Sarah conspired and orchestrated the birth of a son.

Remember this: If God didn't create it, He is not obligated to bless it! He won't bless your mess, but... He will turn your mess into a miracle!

The good news is that in all of His wisdom, God somehow looks beyond our infirmities, iniquities and flaws and sees you as a person worth dying for and being loved and respected and cherished.

Throughout the Bible the Father calls us His children, His beloved, His sons and daughters, His seed, My people and His heirs. Believe it or not... our prosperity is tied to our relationship with Him. It is a prosperity that was promised long before we were even born. Healing is tied to our relationship with our Heavenly Father. It was paid IN FULL at Calvary. Deliverance is tied to our relationship with Him. It was implemented when we accepted Jesus Christ as Lord and personal Savior.

SECTION I

CLEARLY DEFINED

―――――― ❊ ――――――

E very relationship (with God or man) must be clearly defined in order for the relationship to continue and grow. Misjudging the nature of any relationship can lead you to be frustrated, misunderstood, hurt, angry, or disappointed.

In Matthew 16:13-20, Jesus knows that the future of Christianity rests on the revelation Peter has of the Christ. I believe all of Heaven stood poised, anticipating Peter's answer. If he gives the wrong answer, Jesus would have to look for someone else who has received the revelation of who He really is If he answers correctly, then Jesus could bestow authority, access and power to Peter and the others. Notice that it doesn't matter who other men say He is; what is most important here is that Peter has a clear definition of who Jesus is.

Thankfully Peter answers correctly. Notice Jesus' response (verse 17-19):

> *"Blessed are you Simon Bar-jona: for flesh and blood hath not revealed it to thee but my Father which is in heaven. And I say also unto thee, That thou art Peter, and upon this rock I will build my church; and the gates of hell shall not prevail against it. And I will give unto thee the keys of the Kingdom of Heaven: and whatso-ever thou shalt bind on earth shall be bound*

in heaven: and whatsoever thou shalt loose on
earth shall be loosed in heaven."

Jesus could not empower nor entrust Peter with the keys to the Kingdom of Heaven (signifying access), nor give him a new name, signifying covenant, and authority to bind and loose, signifying power, without first clearly defining the nature of their relationship. Peter's answer also speaks to our generation. I can see why the Catholic Church puts so much emphasis on Peter, making him their first bishop-he was the first one to clearly articulate the clear definitions between us and our Savior, *"Thou art the Christ."*

The church, however, is built on revelation, not on the man. God gives revelation continually as we continue to pursue a relationship with Him. This is why prayer and worship are so important. It puts us in a continual posture to pursue Him.

Every relationship that is alive and growing goes through change. When one party changes and the other party refuses to change, that relationship is in jeopardy of being weakened. In your Christian walk, you should be changing from glory to glory and from faith to faith, day by day.

Consider the martyrs in early Christendom; when they faced death, they would honorably lay down their lives for the relationship and the furtherance of the gospel. They would endure humiliation and persecution for the sake of the relationship, not as a good work or a noble deed.

Many Christians believe that their relationship with God does not need to be developed or be clearly manifested to the public once they arrive at a certain level of maturity. So let me help dispel a churchy notion. Just because a person goes to church on a Sunday morning or does volunteer work at the church does not substitute for the one-on-one times God wants to spend with you. Most people I know who are doing well in ministry, marriage, or career are open to having a continual openness in expressing the nature of their relationship with others.

I believe everyone reading this book should at one point or another confirm their relationship with God. Have you confessed Him as your personal Lord and Savior? *Are you His child or not?* It is time to settle the matter. Ambiguously defined relationships usually result in someone getting hurt or disappointed.

> *"...Not everyone that saith Lord, Lord, shall inherit the kingdom of heaven; but he that doeth the will of my Father which is in heaven. Many will say in that day, Lord, Lord, have we not prophesied in thy name? And in thy name cast out devils? And in thy name done many wonderful works? And then I will profess unto them, **I never knew you**: depart from me, ye that work iniquity"*. Matthew 7:21-23

This scripture alone makes it pretty clear that it is possible for a person to cast out devils, prophesy, and do wonderful works and miss the opportunity to go to heaven. **How?** By never coming into a true, clearly defined relationship with the Father.

Have you ever looked through the Bible and noticed how many times God would say, *"I am the Lord thy God,"* or "*I will be their God, and they will be my people*"? Many times He will remind us of who He is and the relationship He wants with us <u>before</u> He gives a command, speaks through a prophet, or performs a miracle. He will make declarative statements like, "I AM (whatever you need Him to be)"; He will first clearly establish who He is to us.

On a more practical note, take the case of a young man or woman who misunderstood the nature of their relationship. Statements like, "I just wanted to be your friend," or "I thought you loved me" or the classic line from the '70's, "I love you so much that I am willing to let you go," are usually spoken by those who have missed the mark on defining the nature of their relationship. Failure to clearly define basic relationships in day-to- day living can result in unwanted pregnancies, abuse and mistrust. If a young engaged couple does not clearly define their relationship on a continual basis, they deny themselves the opportunity to solidify the foundation of their impending marriage.

Throughout the book, we will explore social environments common to most of us to see the importance of clearly defining the relationships around us. And in each environment, let's ask the question, "WHO are you and WHY are you in my life at this time?"

LET'S GO TO CHURCH

How many times has misjudging the church relationship between a pastor and a member led to disappointment or an unrepentant early exit from church membership? I cannot tell you how many times I have had Christians come into my office who are not members of my church to discuss an issue. One of the first questions I will ask is, *"Have you discussed this matter with your pastor?"* Eighty percent of the respondents say, "No!" For any number of reasons, Christians will not turn to their own clergy person for an answer; they would rather go to someone else to discuss the sensitive matter instead of taking it to their clergyman, the person who God has ordained to pray for them and shepherd their soul. If you're not careful, this type of dynamic can backfire on you because it crosses the line of spiritual authority and relationships, between the pastor and member and between one pastor to another pastor.

Are you easily impressed by the outward demonstrated spirituality of someone in your church? I used to be, but not any longer. I have learned over the years that everything that glitters is not gold. Every person that walks into my church declaring how much they can do, and what they know, can deceive even the most seasoned church leader.

When new ministers come into our church to register their spiritual gift, they should be allowed a certain period of time to transition before using them or giving them any responsibility. This season is given to them to allow relationship to be developed. Because we live in a performance-based society, people will come into the church with high ambition to do things, and if they have not caught the heart of the pastor nor the vision of the church, they can actually hinder the effectiveness of the ministry or misuse the authority given to them and cause hurt.

In our church, my wife and I make it a point to try to meet every new member that connects with our ministry. We try to sit in every New Members class (as time permits) and explain in no uncertain terms the vision for the church and what is deemed as appropriate or inappropriate behavior. It may come across as being strict or too straightforward, but in these days of deception, I believe it is important to clearly define church membership roles and operational procedures so that there is no room for offense.

I make it clear that expectations placed on us go both ways. I tell them that if it is unethical for the reverend (me) to have a girlfriend on the side, drink, party, do drugs, smoke and lie, the same holds true for them.

The bottom line question is, "Am I <u>your</u> pastor?" Within the church there are three levels of relationships that are analogous to the tabernacle (Outer Court, Inner Court and Holy of Holies). I have the congregation or general assembly (Outer Court), the membership, (Inner Court) and the staff (Holy of Holies). It is important for pastors to know the difference; otherwise, you will be set up for disappointment and discouragement.

There are matters of responsibility and confidentiality that are imparted into Inner court staff people that Outer court congregation people are not given. In terms of support and commitment, staff members are expected to take the lead in doing those things that I have shared with them in staff meetings or in-gatherings.

Pastors must realize that they may not be the pastor for everyone who visits or comes into their church. Some people who come to your church regularly only come to say, "Amen," feel good and be friendly, but as soon as a strong word is ministered, or a challenge is presented, they disappear and will strangely reappear when the challenge has left. You cannot place much investment in them because the foundation of the relationship is surface and cannot withstand anything more than curiosity and pleasantries.

Things like tithing, consistent attendance in Bible study or Intercessory Prayer, and faithfully serving, can become benchmarks to determine their commitment and loyalty, before any further expectation is manifested. Once a visitor senses a "spiritual connection," and has embraced the vision of the church, the heart of the pastor, and the spirit of the house, they are then ready to make the next step toward membership. For some, it is almost immediate, for others, it takes a while for them to be comfortable enough to embrace the heart of the church.

Membership people are those who have embraced a deeper relationship that is more consistent. They call you "Pastor" and have an expectation for hearing the voice of the pastor. Jesus said,

> "...The sheep follow him, for they know his voice, and a stranger will they not follow, but will flee from him; for they know not the voice of strangers". John 10:3, 4

As they connect, their personal pronouns change from *that* church, to *my* church; from *that* pastor to *my* pastor and from what *they* are doing to what *we* are doing. They become more open to the worship and their work in the ministry is not as inconsistent as it used to be. They can embrace the vision of the local church and are open to serve and participate and be a part of the exciting things going on in the church. We often say "If you want to be a part, you must do your part!"

Have you ever heard the statement that in most churches, "twenty percent of the people do eighty percent of the work, and give eighty percent of the financial support of the ministry"? It's true! As unfortunate as it may be, the reality is that until a person can wholeheartedly embrace the ministry as theirs, they normally will not make an investment beyond the definition of the relationship. Matthew 6:21 says,

> *"For where your treasure is, there will your heart be also."*

I have noticed over the years that when members get offended (for whatever reason), one of the first things to be withheld is their giving. This is because their heart toward the relationship of the ministry has changed, so consequently their investment will follow.

The third group is your staff (paid or volunteer) members (Holy of Holies)-those trusted members in the church who have assumed certain responsibilities to support the work of the ministry. Every elder, deacon, trustee, board member, auxiliary, and minister must clearly define the relationship among themselves as well as those above or beneath them. Deacons don't run the church, and board members don't dictate what the pastor should or should not preach! The role of the pastor is clearly defined in Jeremiah 3:15, which says,

> *"And I will give you pastors according to mine heart, which shall feed you with knowledge and understanding."*

16

In the church, people are intricately connected to support one another and worship together, just as the human body is interconnected. Ephesians 4:6 says,

> "*From whom the whole body fitly joined together and compacted by that which every joint supplieth, according to the effectual working in the measure of every part, maketh increase of the body unto the edifying of itself in love.*"

When people get excited and throw out blanket statements like, "I love you," to me, I take it for what it is worth based on our clearly defined relationship. In Luke 6:46, Jesus says,

> "*And why call ye me Lord, Lord, and do not the things which I say?*"

I say, why say you love me, when our relationship is not at that level yet? Jesus said, "*If you love me, keep my commandments.*" It is important to establish trust in a relationship, before saying such things.

Thankfully, the Bible gives several different definitions for the word "Love."

WILLINGLY EMBRACED

---- ❈ ----

John 15:4 says, "Abide in me, and I in you. As the branch cannot bear fruit of itself, except it abide in the vine; no more can ye, except ye abide in me."
Once the purpose of a relationship has been clearly defined, the next step is to <u>Willingly Embrace</u> the relationship-not grudgingly but willingly. The Father has designed our success and prosperity according to our ability to embrace His Will. The more we embrace Him, trust Him and agree with Him, the more He proves Himself strong on our behalf. This chapter will deal the with Principle of Agreement, how to overcome offenses, and key roles men and women play in the family.

I will go out on a limb here by telling you that saying "No," to God will limit your effectiveness as a leader and will cut off your availability to be blessed by Him. I believe firmly that people who are blessed by the Lord don't tell God, "No." They have somehow tapped into the profound truth that God has a plan charged with prosperity for our lives; all we have to do is say, "Yes, Lord," and agree with Him, and wonderful things will begin to happen. I will use one simple story in the Bible to express this thought.

A GIRL NAMED MARY

One of my favorite examples is the encounter young Mary had with the angel announcing that she would conceive a child (Luke 2). This is not just a Christmas story. It is our story! In Luke 1:28, the angel greets her by saying, "Hail, (1) Thou art highly favored, (2) The Lord is with thee, (3) Blessed art thou among women.

> (v29) And when she saw him she was troubled at his saying and cast in her mind what manner of salutation this should be. And before she could say anything to talk her way out of this moment, the angel says (v30) Fear not, Mary: for thou hast found favor with God."

The reason I say this story is not just a Christmas story is purely hermeneutical. I believe she had not been greeted like that very often. She was a poor girl from the "not so good part of town" and she was in love with and just married a young man who did not have a lot to offer her. I wonder if Mary knew that she was highly favored of God <u>before</u> the angel visited her.

FOUR THINGS THE ANGEL SAID TO MARY
(and will say to us!) Luke 2:28-30

1. *Thou art highly favored of God* (even if you don't feel like it).
2. *The Lord is with thee* (even if it doesn't seem like it).

3. *You are blessed among women.* (even though your conditions don't appear that way).
4. *Fear not* (even though you have no idea of the magnitude of what is about to happen in your life).

The first obstacle was overcoming fear and doubt. God was not going to allow fear–whether it is fear of success, her past, or what the townspeople would think of her–to preempt His plan for the redemption of mankind.

FOUR THINGS MARY SAID BACK TO THE ANGEL
(Luke 2:34, 38, 46)

1. *How can this be?* This is the typical response when God drops a kingdom dynamic in your heart. The answer however will always be the same–THE HOLY GHOST. It is here where she contends with the will to embrace something greater than herself.
2. *Behold, the handmaid of the Lord.* I believe Mary is starting to catch ahold of the fact that God can and will make a miracle of her mess! I can imagine her saying to herself, "I don't know how I'm going to explain this to Joseph but... with God nothing shall be impossible (v37), so let's do it!" Here she is putting herself in a position to be blessed.
3. *Be it unto me according to thy Word.* Praise God, she got it! She embraces God's will for her life. This was the statement that sent the angel back to Heaven. Mission accomplished! When Mary got in faith to agree, even though she had no way of knowing how this would unfold in her life, she set in motion a divine relationship that would cause

21

her name to be remembered every time the gospel is preached.

This same type of dynamic can happen to every person who reads this book. God will select you, and <u>before</u> He tells you what He is going to do in your life while telling you what you mean to Him. He will comfort you with an understanding that says, "I am with you," and that you are "blessed among women." All this, <u>before</u> He tells you what He is going to tell you, so you don't disqualify yourself because of your past life experiences and defeatism.

See, some people have to be convinced that God can use them-even with their faults, flaws, insecurities and bad habits. Notice that He didn't give her a chance to speak, before He said, "Fear not." He knew that she would respond in fear and talk herself right out of her divine destiny, just like many of us would do.

When Mary said, *"Be it unto me according to thy Word"*, (v38), she was uttering the same words God longs for us to say when He wants us to respond to Him!

It takes faith to willingly embrace such an invitation because many times, it is too profound for what we experience in everyday living. There are times when God will speak to you with such clarity and vision for something that it may startle you, but the witness to do what He has shown you has to be confirmed through others.

After Mary accepted what was about to happen in her life, she went to her pregnant cousin Elizabeth's house.

> *"And it came to pass, that when Elizabeth heard the salutation of Mary, the babe leaped in her womb and Elizabeth was filled with the*

Holy Ghost and said, "Blessed art thou among women, and blessed is the fruit of thy womb." (v45) And blessed is she that believed: for there shall be a performance of those things which were told her from the Lord." Luke 1:39-42

I believe that Elizabeth was the Confirming Witness to encourage Mary that another Divine Relationship was about to be birthed. Notice that Elizabeth used almost the exact wording that the angel used (compare v28 and v42). With each confirmation, it becomes a little easier to accept challenges and relationships with God and others that would otherwise be difficult to embrace.

4. *My soul does magnify the Lord, and my spirit hath rejoiced in God my Savior.*

"For He has regarded the low estate of His hand-maiden for, behold, for behold, from henceforth all generations shall call me blessed."

Luke 1:46-47

Not a bad statement for a young, poor girl from the impoverished side of town. This is where the manifestation or the demonstration of what she received is being boldly proclaimed. The rest of her story is known to everyone. She conceived a son, named Him Jesus and even to this day, her story is as popular as any other story in the entire Bible and has been told to children from generation to generation in practically every language on the planet.

IN THE WORKPLACE

When I was in the military, there were fraternization rules and regulations that were strictly enforced by senior officers and enlisted members. At first, I did not understand the reasoning; to me, people were people, they just had more rank than I did, but that did not make them better than me, nor did it prevent me from doing my job. Those rules were not just for peacetime but for wartime (as it was explained to me in no uncertain terms). During times of battle, your response should be, "Yes, Sir, or Yes, Ma'am," to those who were in authority over you. So if or when your commander says, "Take the hill" or "Move out", it is never for debate or conversation. Lives are at stake and you could place others in jeopardy because of the social relationship that existed prior to the command.

In the corporate business environment, the same is true; it may not be lives, but it could result in loss of a client or an account. Employees and managers need to willingly embrace their position or status in order for harmony to occur. Unless those above you grant you permission to call them by their first name or certain liberties to do things, I recommend keeping things formal and professional. Realize, of course, that once permission is granted toward the informal, it is difficult to go back to being formal.

As difficult as it may seem, each role, title, or position must be willingly embraced. There may be times when you work with a peer that you don't get along with. It is vitally important that you embrace the fact that you two just don't get along. There is no need to force the issue; simply agree that you don't agree and move on! It takes a secure person to do this because it may be your nature to want everyone to get along with you because you are a wonderful person. The reality is that sometimes God places people in your life to get on your last nerve! They come to strengthen your patience and longsuffering.

I have come to the conclusion that I don't fit in with everyone; I wasn't designed that way...and it's okay! I was always a little different that way. This is a way to overcome being offended. You will not always be included in their party or invited to sit at the "cool kids table".

FREELY INVESTED IN

---- ❋ ----

Any relationship left to itself will eventually grow stale and dry if it is not invested in. Like anything else that God has created and is alive, it rests on the **Principle of Respiration** discussed later in this book. For any healthy relationship to continue and grow, there has be investments made into it. Whether it be time, money, presence, or words, every relationship requires some sort of investment. Gary Chapman, in his book *The Five Love Languages* lists: Words of Affirmation, Gifts, Acts of Service, Physical Touch and Time, as necessary investments for every couple to continue thriving.

I encourage the reader to pick one, any one of these types of investments to sow into your family, church, or department and watch some amazing results take place.

For any person wanting to better understand the relationships orchestrated by God to bless your life, I give this one simple word…NEVER make an investment that goes beyond the definition of your relationship.

We recently took our grandkids to Hawaii for the first time. It was expensive, but boy, was it worth it! Their excitement of being smashed by waves, making sand castles, and the freedom to laugh out loud was priceless! We believe that making this kind of investment will leave a lasting memory in their young minds for a very long time.

WORDS WE LIVE BY

- Every relationship (with God or man) must be CLEARLY DEFINED in order for the relationship to continue and grow.
- When people get excited and throw out blanket statements like, "I love you," to me, I take it for what it is worth based on our clearly defined relationship.
- Once the purpose of a relationship has been clearly defined, the next step is to WILLINGLY EMBRACE the relationship-not grudgingly but willingly.
- The Father has designed our success and prosperity according to our ability to embrace His will. The more we embrace Him, trust Him and agree with Him, the more He proves Himself strong on our behalf.
- God will select you, and before He tells you what He is going to do in your life, while telling you what you mean to Him. Our job is to Willingly Embrace what His assignment is for our lives!
- Any relationship left to itself will eventually grow stale and dry, if it is not invested in like anything else that God has created and is alive. For any healthy relationship to continue and grow, there has be investments made into it. Whether it be time, money, presence, or words, every relationship requires some sort of investment.

SECTION II

———— ✳ ————

EMBRACING SONSHIP

———— ❄ ————

The idea that God is just a miracle-working anomaly existing only in the celestial outer-atmosphere is a ridiculous notion. I have discovered that the Bible is not only a book of history, geography, poetry, and science, but it is a book of genealogy and relationships.

The Bible story is basically about a Father who created an environment for His children who have abandoned their heritage, lineage and inheritance only to be reconciled by their elder brother Jesus Christ, who was the WORD OF GOD transformed to become flesh and live a sinless life, who made the ultimate sacrifice of His own life, and then returned to the Father to intercede on our behalf while sending the Holy Spirit to dwell in the hearts of men to alert them if they every went astray again!

Someone once said, THE SON OF GOD BECAME THE SON OF MAN, SO THAT THE SONS OF MEN COULD BECOME SONS OF GOD! I believe this is a true statement especially when you consider what Jesus imparted to us through His death, burial, and resurrection.

Some people have no idea that Jesus came to fulfill all the promises that the Old Testament prophets could only imagine and hope for! Because of the shed blood of Jesus Christ, we now have access into a family that ensures we have all the blessings of Abraham, Isaac, and Jacob!

Throughout the Scriptures God shows us relationships that depict mentorship, discipleship and more.

My pastor, the late Apostle Nathaniel Holcomb, has established an entire school of ministry just based on the dynamic of Sonship; the school is called Sonship School of the Firstborn.

This school within the church is designed to transform people from a Servant mentality to a Son mentality. It is modeled after the relationship of Elijah and Elisha, as found in II Kings 2.

As we began this school in our church several years ago, we literally saw spiritual transformation and maturation taking place in the lives of the students year after year. The question of "spiritual formation" was answered in every section of the course as students discovered the "_Why_ we do _what_ we do", during church services. One of the key discoveries during the entire course is helping people discover their spiritual gifts. Just as Elisha picked up the mantle of Elijah, we encourage students to pick up their gift, talents, abilities and anointing to discover what the Father has given to them–simply because they are discovering a divine relationship with Him.

> Consider this scripture found in I John 3:1, 2, "*Behold, what manner of love the Father hath bestowed upon us, that we should be called the Sons of God: therefore the world knoweth us not, because it knew him not. Beloved, now are we the Sons of God, and it doth not yet appear what we shall be: but we know that, when he shall appear, we shall be like him; for we shall see him as he is.*"

The word **Sonship-**comes from two words…

<u>SON</u> – because we are made His children through the spiritual adoption process that came with salvation.

<u>SHIP</u> – because are made kinship to Him (even though we did not qualify due to race and creed or nationality). We were grafted into this relationship.

Romans 11:17 (NLT) puts it this way:

> *But some of these branches from Abraham's tree – some of the people of Israel – have been broken off. And you Gentiles, who were branches from a wild olive tree, have been grafted in. So now you also receive the blessing God has promised Abraham and his children, sharing in the rich nourishment from the root of God's special olive tree.*

What a great blessing it is to know that being made a part of a relationship with God is like one plant being grafted in with another plant to form and uniquely designed individual called *"Me."*

The word *father* conjures up different images for everyone. To some, it brings the picture of love, laughter, respect and acceptance. Unfortunately, others associate the term *father* with fear, rejection, disappointment, and intimidation.

That is why it is so important to <u>not</u> to take your understanding of your Heavenly Father from the experiences of others or social media–TAKE IT FROM THE SCRIPTURES.

You undoubtedly had an imperfect earthly father like I did, perhaps one who brought you harm physically or absenteeism. The good news is that God is the model of a Father in the truest sense of the Word.

Matthew 11:27 (MSG) Jesus said to the people, *"The Father has given me all these things to do and say. This is a unique Father-Son operation, coming out of Father and Son intimacies and knowledge. No one knows the Son the way the Father does, nor does the Father the way of the Son. But I'm not keeping it to myself; I'm ready to go over it line by line with anyone willing to listen."*

Throughout the Bible, the paternal order of Sonship speaks to our posterity. Every man and woman, regardless of age, should embrace the concept of being a Son to somebody. It is not limited to biology or skin color. It is really about a relationship dynamic that God has established to bring love, peace, order, security and blessings into a person's life. In the natural we have coaches, mentors, pastors, and life-coaches in our lives to advise us, push us, and challenge us to do better in life!

This allows someone who you respect to speak into your life, and because we don't know everything, God blesses us with people of integrity and love to help us avoid many of lifes' pitfalls and traps.

We all need someone to <u>correct us</u> when we make a mistake and <u>bless us</u> like no one else can. Sometimes it's a word that can be strong and direct. Nevertheless, truth stands on its own foundation.

I taught my sons that the greatest thing a dad can do is… BE THERE! Any father figure knows the value of attending a ball game, a school play or a significant moment in a child's life.

Every Christian ought to know the voice of their Heavenly Father, which can be a guiding light in a world filled with too many deflected truths.

One day after an awesome Sunday service seven year-old Ajiah greeted me, and we laughed and hugged, but when she heard her daddy's voice in the midst of our over-crowded church foyer, she abruptly cut our conversation off and ran toward his voice before she could even see him. *How rude!* I thought to myself. But what a life lesson! I hope we all can do that in life –run to the Father when we hear His voice!

Jesus was the perfect Son. **While on earth Jesus <u>never</u> took on the posture of being a Father**. He always positioned Himself to be a Son (with the authority of His Father). His goal and role was always to bring humanity back into a right relationship with the Heavenly Father. Let's peek into a conversation between Phillip and Jesus in John 14:8-14 (MSG)

> *Philip said, "Master, show us the Father; then we'll be content." Jesus said, "You've been with me all this time, Philip, and you <u>still</u> don't understand? To see me <u>is</u> to see the Father. So how can you ask, 'Where is the Father?' Don't you believe that I am in the Father and the Father is in me? The words that I speak to you aren't mere words. I don't just make them up on my own. The Father who resides in me crafts each word into a divine act. "Believe me: I am in my Father and my Father is in me. If you can't believe that, believe what you see — these works. The person who trusts me will not only do what I'm doing but even greater*

*things, because I, on my way to the Father, am
giving you the same work to do that I've been
doing. You can count on it. From now on, whatever you request along the lines of who I am and
what I am doing, I'll do it. That's how the Father
will be seen for who he is in the Son. I mean it.
Whatever you request in this way, I'll do.*

Basically, this scripture is saying, *"Like Father, like Son."*
Jesus is the way that leads to a divine relationship with the
Father, which includes all the rights, benefits, and privileges
the Jews had through Abraham, Isaac and Jacob.

In Ephesians 1:3-14, the Apostle Paul writes with exu-
berant joy as he shares a great revelation with the saints in
the city of Ephesus while he is in prison. In two over-ex-
tended, compound-complex sentences, Paul expresses the
vast and almost indescribable riches of redemption that
God has provided for us as our inheritance through Jesus
Christ. He uses phrases like: He has "Blessed Us", "Chosen
Us," "Predestinated Us", "Accepted Us", and "Sealed Us"
into the beloved.

This pericope expresses that no longer would the Jews
be the only ones to have exclusive rights and access to
God. The GOOD NEWS is that now Gentiles (anyone who
is not of the Jewish faith) can have the same blessing of
God's grace and not only that...but Salvation is available
to everyone and anyone through the adoption of Sonship
through Jesus Christ.

The reality of this scripture came to me recently when I
met little Daniel for the first time; he was eight months old.
He was born to a drug-addicted mother who already had
to give up her four-year-old daughter Eboni earlier because

her addiction would not allow her to keep the children. Eboni was born pre-mature and now little Daniel has been diagnosed with a Level 6 heart murmur (he has a hole in his heart) and needs to be seen by a pediatric cardiologist.

Under normal circumstances this would be a lose-lose situation, but thanks to Tony and Brook Davis, there is hope for both children. Tony and Brook went through the legal battles and procedures to legally adopt Eboni and Daniel as one of their very own! The medical benefits provided for the Davis family now covered Eboni and little Daniel. The beauty of this story is that even though Tony and Brook are Caucasian and Eboni and Daniel are light-skinned African-American children, THEY ARE NOW FAMILY!

All this was made possible because long before Daniel was born, an adoption process was created whereby Daniel could be adopted and receive the care he would eventually need so he could live a normal life in a healthy family. What a blessing!

I share this story because just like little Eboni and Daniel, we all had a "spiritual hole in our heart" that only Jesus could fill. We all needed the love and care that comes by way of "Adoption as Sons," where regardless of race and gender, we can receive the benefits of being in the family of God through Jesus Christ.

One more story on the topic of Sonship. When I was in graduate school, we were required to exegete Ephesians Chapter One. I stayed up late in the library digging out as much information as I could regarding the vast blessing in this powerful chapter when I stumbled upon a book entitled, "*Sonship Theology*." What? A theology based on Sonship? I never heard of such a thing...but it was certainly worth exploring.

Basically, Sonship Theology was a practiced belief that Christians were adopted as children of God and no longer had to hold tenants of rules and restrictions within a certain denomination. However, to my utter amazement, this stirred a great controversy within that denomination that Christians, as believers had rights–Sonship rights while others in that same denomination believed that these rights and privileges were only for those "called" into the ministry.

The Christian life through Sonship is not solely a commandment-orientated way of life, where people are robotic and religious, nor is it free-lanced Christianity where people simply "let go" and do as they please; no, it is a lifestyle of effort, application and balance to what the Word of God has already declared.

Sonship Rights are promises in the Word of God that are available to us because we are Sons of God through Salvation. They are available because of what God has done in Christ Jesus. We cannot earn Sonship Rights, and all sons, just like in your family, get the SAME rights. We do not have to do anything to claim them, except to accept Jesus Christ as your Lord and Personal Savior. We simply must believe God's Word and act upon it literally. The New Testament is our legal document that declares our rights as sons of the One and True God.

Just as we are beneficiaries to certain rights and privileges as citizen of the United States, consider this opening pre-amble to the Declaration of Independence,

> *"We hold these truths to be self-evident, that all*
> *men are created equal, that they are endowed by*
> *their Creator with certain unalienable Rights,*

that among these are Life, Liberty and the pursuit of Happiness."

The New Testament is written in the blood of Jesus Christ. God almighty sealed it as something unprecedented in Jewish history. He gave every redeemed believer the rights and blessings the Jews enjoyed for thousands of years. Not only that, but God gave His Sons the power and authority through Jesus Christ as He planned to give man before the creation of the heavens and the earth (Gen. 1:26-28).

This was such a critical issue that the Apostle Paul was thrown in jail for proclaiming this life-changing truth. In 1483, Martin Luther wrote in his *95 Theses*, (which eventually led to the Protestant Reformation) that believers no longer needed an intermediary and strict adherence to the pope and the king. He cried… *"Sola Scriptura* (by Scripture alone)"*, "Sola Fida* (Faith alone)"*, "Sola Gratia* (Grace alone)"*, "Sola Christo* (Christ alone)" and *"Sola Deo Gloria* (Glory to God alone)."*

For this, Martin Luther (the Great Reformer) was declared to be an outlaw; his literature was banned and the authorities requiring his arrest stated *"We want him to be apprehended and punished as a* notorious heretic."* They also made it a crime for anyone in Germany to give Luther food or shelter. Lastly, they permitted anyone to kill Luther without legal consequence.

WORDS WE LIVE BY

- What a great blessing it is to know that being made a part of a relationship with God is like one plant being grafted in with another plant to form and uniquely designed individual called "Me."

- It is so important to not to take your understanding of your Heavenly Father from the experiences of others or social media – TAKE IT FROM THE SCRIPTURES
- Every man and woman, regardless of age, should embrace the concept of being a Son to somebody. It is not limited to biology or skin color. It is really about a relationship dynamic that God has established to bring love, peace, order, security and blessings into a person's life.
- The Father has a need that only we (as His children) can fulfill. In all His omnipotence, His omnipresence, and His omniscience, He has a need, and that need is to have His children reconciled to Him
- Sonship Rights are promises in the Word of God that are available to us because we are Sons of God through Salvation. They are available because of what God has done in Christ Jesus. We cannot earn Sonship Rights, and all sons, just like in your family, get the SAME rights.

SECTION III

GENESIS PRINCIPLES

--------- ✳ ---------

I n defining Divine Relationships, I believe that God ascribed biblical principles that are inherent in nature to help us better understand relationship dynamics. In Romans 1:20 we find, *"For the invisible things of him from creation are clearly seen, being understood by the things that are made…"* The Message Bible helps us understand this a bit more clearly by stating,

> *"Open your eyes and there it is! By taking a long and thoughtful look at what God has created, people have always been able to see what their eyes as such can't see: eternal power, for instance, and the mystery of his divine being. So nobody has a good excuse."*

When you look at the book of Genesis closely, you will discover a neatly woven theme that communicates God's heart toward His greatest creation–Us! And you will discover the way to establish and maintain healthy relationships in and around your own life!

At the risk of sounding redundant, the Rules of Engagement in understanding these Genesis Principles and their application are provided here:

1. Genesis Principles work harmoniously with all the other principles with other principles described

later in this book. So, there is a direct co-relation between *The Principle of Seed Time and Harvest* and the *Principle of Agreement* for example. As you read about one, you will discover that other principles are woven into each other.

2. God is a God of relationships; so everything that He created and is alive operates in association with something else; no thing and no one that is alive was created to exist by itself.

The caveat to this is in the wording throughout this book is the phrase, "CREATED BY GOD AND IS ALIVE." If God did not create it–He is not responsible for its condition and outcome; and if it is not alive, the principles don't apply, nor do they apply to dead relationships or inanimate objects. For example, if a person is in a dysfunctional, abusive, or flat-lined relationship that He did not assign you to, He is not obligated to bless that relationship… unless there is a significant change. He only blesses what He creates!

As I have counseled many young adults over the years about their hurts and disappointments one common thread was that the two should never have been together in the first place! Secondly, whether it was hormonal, desperation, or simply missing the voice of God (or other divinely appointed people), when two people get married without proper counsel, it usually ends with one party getting hurt, emotionally scarred, or defensive toward the next opportunity for any relationship to develop. WHY? Because the relationship was created in an atmosphere that was not conducive for fruitfulness.

PRINCIPLE & POWER
OF PROCESS

In the beginning God created the heavens and the earth. And the earth was without form and void and darkness was upon the face of the deep. And the Spirit of God moved upon the face of the waters… And God said, Let there be light: and there was light. And God saw the light, that it was good: and God divided the light from the darkness. And God called the light Day, and the darkness he called Night. And the evening and the morning were the first day. And God said, let there be a firmament in the midst of the waters and let it divide the waters which were under the firmament from the waters which were above the firmament; and it was so. Genesis 1:1-7.

According to Dictionary.com, a process is defined as a *systematic series of actions directed toward some end or leads to a particular result.*

This Genesis simply states that every healthy relationship created by God must undergo a process in order for the relationship to continue and grow.

Can you imagine…planet Earth being in a state of shapelessness, a chaotic mass of formlessness, no order, but ALIVE with all the energy and potential of what we know it to be today?

The term *"Firmament"* is almost incomprehensible to many people and is often an argument by theologians over its definition. The word simply means, "expansion." It denotes the space or expanse like an arch appearing immediately above us. Like the difference between stratosphere (upper) and mesosphere (lower), God had to systematically implement a process to separate the things of nature in order to create and atmosphere suitable for man to live in.

Journey back in time with me to an era I will call *"the dateless past."* The upper regions and earth were in total disarray. They were *"without form,"* means chaotic, like a wilderness and *"void"* means empty like a wasteland; and *"darkness"* which means not just lacking light but it was obscure, meaning incomprehensibility vague, murky and ambiguous.

When God *(Elohim)* looked at the condition of the world, He HAD TO do something! Like a great architect and master planner, He created and formed a world with His divine plan and purpose for mankind in mind.

Here's the process in action…He made firmaments to separate the waters and established a system or structure we commonly call an eco-system, but it was more than that…He set in order *The Principle & Power of Process*. Because His nature is to be orderly, all of what we see and know about Him is <u>structural and orderly,</u> even at the deepest ocean floor or the highest height of our solar system; but be certain…it is especially true in relationships.

Arbitrary, vague, and formless relationships are not His design for any of us! Notice who was NOT there in the creation process...Adam and Eve. Even though *Elohim* had Adam in His mind from the very beginning, He could not create Adam until the atmosphere was set for him to "have dominion". There was no garden! Look at Genesis 1:27, 28

> *"And God said, Let us make man in our image, after our likeness: and let them have dominion over the fish of the sea, and over the fowl of the air, and over the cattle, and over all the earth, and over every creeping thing that creepeth upon the earth. So God created man in his own image, in the image of God created he him; male and female created he them.*
>
> *And God blessed them, and God said unto them, Be fruitful, and multiply, and replenish the earth, and subdue it: and have dominion over the fish of the sea, and over the fowl of the air, and over every living thing that moves upon the earth.*

Like Adam and Eve, we are all created in God's image, and we all have a specific *"Life Assignment"* to fulfill. He took such care in designing our environment that nature applauds through what we call *"wonders of the world."* No two people on the entire planet are the same! Retinal eye patterns and fingerprints attest to the fact that we are, as Psalm 139 says, *"fearfully and wonderfully made."*

On a more personal note, if the relationships around you are chaotic, vague, and without form...hold on; Your Heavenly Father will look upon your situation just as He did the creation process and establish a firmament (separation) for you to bring order and stability to your life. He does not want your life to be without form and void and dark. That's not healthy!

Every person and every healthy relationship I know has a testimony, and every testimony involves a <u>process</u>. In order to live a victorious life we MUST complete each phase of our life processes with integrity, character, grace, and style. To cheat or circumvent your challenges, tests, and trials is to cheat yourself out of the validity and credibility of your testimony when you come through it.

There are no bragging rights given to those who run away from every fight, dodge every confrontation, and give themselves excuses as to why they can't finish what they start. Life is not a sprint–it's a marathon, it involves enduring to the end.

The processes of life are intricate, and the bigger the expected result, the more important every step of the process becomes. God sits on the throne of our lives *"working all things out after the counsel of his own will"* (Eph. 1:11). "All things work together for good to those who love the Lord and to those who are called according to His purpose (Rom..8:28). Eph. 1:9 says, "He makes known unto us the mystery of His will, according to His good pleasure <u>which He has purposed in himself.</u>"

Nothing grows or moves without implementing some process to keep it growing or moving. Botanically speaking, *Mycosis* and *Mitosis* work together to keep plant reproduction going; EVERYTHING THAT IS HEALTHY AND ALIVE involves a process–its unavoidable!

I counselled a young man who was in a relationship I thought was toxic. When he called me, he explained how she was never happy, but the sex was GREAT! She didn't want to advance in her career, her family had several abusive relationships in it, and she just was too young to be serious about life. Basically, she wanted to flaunt her good looks and party. He, on the other hand, was ready for more…education, raising a family, getting a better job, start going to church, and living a more productive life.

Argument after argument finally led him to physically relocate. That's when he called me. I told him that the best thing he could have done for himself was to make a break from her, even if it meant leaving the city. Then I casually explained to him the Principle & Power of Process in a Cheesecake restaurant and the insights I gave him set him free! He connected the idea of what God had done in his life was all part of a process that he could get back on track with his Life Assignment.

He recognized that as long as he stayed in that toxic relationship, he could not have dominion, be fruitful, or replenish anything resembling the life he believed God had designed for him!

You will know that you are in a Divine Relationship orchestrated by God because it blesses your life toward betterment and wholeness, as opposed to killing your dreams and holding you back because the other person doesn't want to advance.

Personal Testimony: One thing I love about my wife is that she thinks I'm Superman, Denzel Washington, and Dr. Heathcliff Huxtable all rolled up into one! She never blocks or squashes my dreams or goals…even when I doubt myself, she is right there, believing in me and encouraging me. I think as long as she knows that I am following God to the best of my ability, she can be reassured that even my crazy ideas and visions are not designed to do harm but to do good…she buys into it!

This book is designed to help people know that there is something powerful going on inside of you, and it is so vitality important that you finish your life assignment in a healthy and orderly way; the Bible indicates that we are surrounded with a great cloud of witnesses in the heavens, cheering us on to victory.

As a matter of fact, when you get this concept down inside of your thinking, you will laugh at the chaotic and dysfunctional people around you because you will see things a little differently. Believe it or not, but some people have lives that are so chaotic, void, and without form–they consider it "normal".

Last point…a few years ago, the Philadelphia 76ers of the NBA did the unthinkable. In order to become winners, the 76ers had intentionally been one of the worst teams in professional sports history. And after three years, that strategy had worked. The 76ers have perhaps the brightest future of any team in the NBA.

Their theme *"Trust the Process"*, had become a tough reality for traditional sportscasters and Philadelphia fans. Imagine…losing games on purpose in order to position themselves to capitalize on first- round draft picks for the next few years. This seems unethical and unprofessional and…unprecedented. But…it's working!

I am not saying to lose in life on purpose, but what I am saying is that the sacrifices of life cannot be understood by everyone. The process of sacrifice in life only makes sense to you and people who have been through similar sacrifices.

A dear friend and spiritual brother, who is also a successful business executive, sat down with the youth of our church to encourage them in their educational and career pursuits. What he shared was bewildering to the youth but it was completely understood by the parents... He simply told them, *"Make your sacrifices early in life."*

While in college, he said, "I was a nerd, I had no social life, and not many close friends. My focus was on doing well in my classes and it was a great sacrifice to resist the temptations of socializing on a Georgia Tech campus." In the end, his grades gave him access to greater educational and employment opportunities, which led to increased travel, corporate promotions, and a VERY comfortable lifestyle.

How do you convince people to *Trust the Process* that God is orchestrating your life assignments?

Matthew 13:45-46 says, *"The kingdom of heaven is like unto a merchant man, seeking goodly pearls: Who, when he had found one pearl of great price, went and sold all that he had, and bought it."*

It made no sense, except to the merchant man. Here's his process: He sought the pearls; when he found that one pearl of great price he had a decision to make; He sold all that he had (this makes no sense to outsiders looking in), and he bought it.

Healthy relationships are like that!

Testimony: I remember when I first gave my life to Christ back in the 70's, I told a co-worker that I would start going to Bible Study with him. His name was Mike

Roberts. He was a nerdy, buck-toothed, white kid who was determined to hold me to my word.

Unfortunately, I was about to relocate, and my crew was planning a surprise going away party for me that would last almost the entire weekend. They had the DJ, the fly girls with hot pants and afros, more sangria and drinks we could handle. The place was packed with brothers and hot girls dancing to Donna Summer and Chic doing the Bump.

Around 8p.m. on that Friday night, nerdy Mike Roberts had the boldness to come to the apartment, ring the doorbell carrying what looked like a ten-pound King James Bible. *"Is Ralph here?"*, *"Yeah"*, they answered and called for me. At the time, I was upstairs "entertaining" a certain selected young lady and when I came downstairs, the song *Stop Light* by Parliament-Funkadelic came to a screeching halt. I greeted him at the door, *"Mike, what are doing here? Man, you can't walk up here and disrupt this party man, these brothers will hurt you, dude!"*

Un-phased, Mike spoke up and called me out. *"YOU SAID that if I came to get you, you would go with me to Bible study tonight, I did my part, now you have to do yours!"* *Oh Crap!* (I thought to myself... an unexpected defining moment).

Totally embarrassed, I walked pass my crew, went upstairs, said good night to my "special guest," grabbed my old paperback Oral Robert Bible given to me by my mother and humbly walked through the crowd (who were all in total shock as you could imagine), and I went with Mike Roberts to Bible study as I promised.

Ugh...what a sacrifice I had to make that night! No one could understand why I did what I did... but Jesus was my Pearl of Great Price that night. I had to sell all that I might obtain Him!

WORDS WE LIVE BY

- When God (Elohim) looked at the condition of the world, He HAD TO do something! Like a great architect and master planner, He created and formed a world with His divine plan and purpose for mankind in mind.
- If the relationships around you are chaotic, vague, and without form...hold on; Your Heavenly Father will look upon your situation just as He did the creation process and establish a firmament (separation) for you to bring order and stability to your life. He does not want your life to be without form and void and dark. That's just not healthy!
- In order to live a victorious life, we MUST complete each phase of our life processes with integrity, character, grace, and style. To cheat or circumvent your challenges, tests, and trials is to cheat yourself out of the validity and credibility of your testimony when you come through it!
- You will know that you are in a Divine Relationship orchestrated by God because it blesses your life toward betterment and wholeness, as opposed to killing your dreams and holding you back because the other person doesn't want to advance.
- Your sacrifices of life cannot be understood by everyone. The process of sacrifice in life only makes sense to you and people who have been through similar sacrifices.

PRINCIPLE & POWER OF IDENTIFICATION

This principle simply states that everything that God created and is alive has a <u>name and a purpose</u>.

Identification is a MUST in every healthy relationship in order for it to continue to grow and flourish. This principle relates to the point I made earlier about *Clearly Defining* the relationship. In Genesis 1:5, 8, 10 and 2:19, 23, we find the word "*called*" as a recurring theme. The Hebrew word for "Called" is *qara*, which means to give a name to be called, be named, be called out, and be chosen.

This principles states that EVERYTHING THAT GOD CREATED AND IS ALIVE HAS A PURPOSE AND A NAME. Nothing He created is ambiguous and without identification. Here's the pattern: He creates it, establishes its purpose, and He gives it a name.

In Genesis 1:5, we find these words: "And he called the light *Day* and the darkness he called *Night*. He called the firmament *Heaven*, he called the dry lands *Earth*, and the gathering together of the waters He called *Seas*."

It was absolutely imperative that everything God created be given a name and a purpose; otherwise, there will be more confusion and more chaos. He gave light a name called Day, the darkness; He called Night, and then gave them a purpose. He then gave Day and Night a purpose and an assignment; one was greater and the other was lesser, one to rule the day and the other to rule the night.

> Look at Genesis 1:14-18, Then *God said, "Let*
> *there be lights in the firmament of the heavens*
> *to divide the day from the night; and let them*
> *be for signs and seasons, and for days and years;*
> *and let them be for lights in the firmament of the*
> *heavens to give light on the earth"; and it was*
> *so. Then God made two great lights: the greater*
> *light to rule the day, and the lesser light to rule*
> *the night. He made the stars also. God set them*
> *in the firmament of the heavens to give light on*
> *the earth, and to rule over the day and over the*
> *night, and to divide the light from the darkness.*
> *And God saw that it was good.*

Can you see the Great Maestro of Creation putting everything in place with specific assignments which coincide with their existence? This was all done to ensure there would be no chaos or apocalyptic collisions with catastrophic environmental results.

May I submit to you that God had Adam (His first son) in mind while doing this!

When there is a mis-identification in a relationship dynamic, dysfunction, and atrophy will occur. Why? Because when God creates something, it has a name and a purpose. Remember, Adam was not created yet, but when he came on the scene, he was given the authority to name animals and every living creature. Genesis 2:19d says that, "whatever Adam named a thing, THAT was its name", which included Eve (Gen 3:20).

When relationships are defined in vague terms, the relationship is held in a holding pattern. Why? Because the purpose of the relationship is not advancing. Friends can still be friends, as long as the purpose and definition of the relationship is based on <u>friendship</u>. But once emotions or situations change, the definition of the relationship usually follows suit.

It's the reason why dating a co-worker or a client is a slippery slope. The identity of the relationship has to be kept secret or hidden to those on the outside, but the intimacy will ooze out and eventually expose the true feelings of the couple. Ultimately, a redefining of the relationship will be required, or someone will have to find another job!

Interestingly, when a child is still an infant, new parents eagerly want to teach the child to say "Momma" or "Dada," because it is important for the child's development and growth to identify who the parents are!

Consider that after God created Adam (Gen. 1:7), He gave him authority to name all the beasts and fowl and then Chapter 2:19 says...

"... *And whatsoever Adam called every living creature, that was the name thereof.*" Adam took on the likeness, dominion and nature of God Himself by naming the creatures around him... including Eve! (Gen. 2:23).

In today's society, it is easy to see the advantage the devil has in the lives of many people because ambiguity breeds lack of commitment and negates the purpose of the relationship.

> "*When Jesus came into the coasts of Caesarea Philippi, he asked his disciples saying, whom do men say that I the Son of man am? And they said, some say that thou art John the Baptist: some, Elias; and others, Jeremiah or one of the*

prophets. He saith unto them, But whom do ye say that I am? And Simon Peter answered and said, Thou art the Christ, the Son of the Living God." Matthew 16:13-16

Even though we will deal with this scripture later in the book, suffice it to say that Peter's identification of Jesus being the Christ, the Son of the Living God, facilitated his *Kairos* covenant moment. The same will hold true for us when we identify (give a name to) the relationships that surround us.

Whether in the work place, church or home, it is necessary for healthy relationships to have a clear identity. For example, how do you describe the person you are courting? In today's lingo, *"This is my Boo,"* can have so many mis-applications that someone will take it too far or not be willing to go the distance that commitment and sacrifice require.

One of the challenges facing our society is <u>Identification</u>. In our post-modern, post-church, media driven society, it is becoming increasingly more convoluted to place traditional identifications on relationships. Unfortunately, the days of nuclear families are becoming a thing of the past. Today, we have so many types of family structures, I doubt if we will ever see a resurgence of traditional nuclear family structures again.

There is no right or wrong answer when it comes to what is the best type of family structure. As long as a family is filled with love and support for one another, it tends to be successful and thrive. Families need to do what is best for each other and for themselves, and that can be achieved in almost any family unit.

I recently met a few pastors and missionaries who introduced me to a new term called "Pan-sexual" relationships, which is short for a relationship characterized by sexual desire or attraction that is not limited to people of a particular gender identity or sexual orientation. Pansexual people may be sexually attracted to individuals who identify as male or female; however, they may also be attracted to those who identify as inter-sex, third-gender, androgynous, transsexual, or the many other sexual and gender identities.

Their identity for one another is simply, *"Partner,"* which can have so many inferences and outcomes. Even though these types of relationships have existed in certain African countries for hundreds of years as part of their culture, what is taking place in our society is something totally different.

Divine Relationships take their example from what was done during the creation process. Clearly identifiable roles and purposes help relationships to develop and grow–especially those in the traditional sense of the word. Time will tell how the ever-changing names and purposes in relationships will affect the outcome of future generations.

IN THE WORKPLACE

Clearly identifying the roles and responsibilities of peers, co-workers, and superiors is vitality important in order to maintain a healthy work environment. Most successful companies I know have a clear Mission Statement conspicuously posted so that all people associated with that company knows exactly the who, what, how, and why of its existence.

When I need proper customer service or an answer that an associate cannot provide, I immediately ask to speak to a supervisor, manager or as my wife would say, *"I want to speak to someone in charge."* This process is established so that any customer can get the service, answers or support needed to satisfy their concerns...Aren't you glad that a process was already in place to assist you long before you came into the store?

IN THE CHURCH

Church by-laws, Corporate Resolutions, Articles of Incorporation, and other legal documents are established to protect its membership from being another chaotic social environment. This is designed as a process to ensure new members and believers can become part of an organized system of beliefs and practices that lead people to a healthy relationship with God.

I know that we are living in a post-church society where people don't want to embrace "organized religion"; *I get it!* What scares me is a society that is hedonistic, polytheistic, nihilistic, or antithetic because "Order" is viewed as confining or restrictive.

Romans 1:19 – 32 says... *For the wrath of God is revealed from heaven against all ungodliness and unrighteousness of men, who suppress the truth in unrighteousness, because what may be known of God is manifest in them, for God has shown it to them. For since the creation of the world His invisible attributes are clearly seen, being understood by the things that are made, even His eternal power and Godhead, so that they are without excuse, because, although they knew God, they did not glorify Him as God, nor were thankful, but became futile in their thoughts, and their foolish hearts were darkened. Professing to be wise, they became fools, and changed the glory of the incorruptible God into an image made like corruptible man – and birds and four-footed animals and creeping things.*

Therefore God also gave them up to uncleanness, in the lusts of their hearts, to dishonor their bodies among themselves, who exchanged the truth of God for the lie, and worshiped and served the creature rather than the Creator, who is blessed forever. Amen.

For this reason God gave them up to vile passions. For even their women exchanged the natural use for what is against nature. Likewise also the men, leaving the natural use of the woman, burned in their lust for one another, men with men committing what is shameful, and receiving in themselves the penalty of their error which was due. And even as they did not like to retain God in their knowledge, God gave them over to a debased mind, to do those things which are not fitting; being filled with all unrighteousness, sexual immorality, wickedness, covetousness, maliciousness; full of envy,

61

murder, strife, deceit, evil-mindedness; they are whisperers, backbiters, haters of God, violent, proud, boasters, inventors of evil things, disobedient to parents, undiscerning, untrustworthy, unloving, unforgiving,[d] unmerciful; who, knowing the righteous judgment of God, that those who practice such things are deserving of death, not only do the same but also approve of those who practice them.

This scripture tells me that when humankind is left to their own decisions outside of God's Will, there is a great potential toward the moral downfall in that society that I believe will lead to further decay for generations to come.

It is here where I pray for our country and its leaders. I pray that God would give them wisdom to lead according to the way our country was founded and not by what is popular. *"One nation under God, indivisible with liberty and justice for all"* can stand the test of time.

WORDS WE LIVE BY

- Friends can still be friends, as long as the purpose and definition of the relationship is <u>friendship.</u> But once emotions or situations change, the definition of the relationship usually follows suit.
- It's the reason why dating a co-worker or a client is a slippery slope. The identity of the relationship has to be kept secret or hidden to those on the outside, but the intimacy will ooze out and eventually expose the true feelings of the couple. Ultimately,

a redefining of the relationship will be required, or someone will have to find another job!

- Peter's identification of Jesus being the Christ, the Son of the Living God, in Matthew 16:16, facilitated his *Kairos* covenant moment. The same will hold true for us when we identify (give a name to) the relationships that surround us.

- Divine Relationships take their example from what was done during the creation process. Clearly identifiable roles and purposes help relationships to develop and grow–especially those in the traditional sense of the word. Time will tell how the ever-changing names and purposes in relationships will affect the outcome of future generations.

PRINCIPLE & POWER
OF AGREEMENT

> Genesis 1:26-27 says, *"Then God said, "Let*
> *Us make man in Our image, according to Our*
> *likeness; let them have dominion over the fish*
> *of the sea, over the birds of the air, and over the*
> *cattle, over all the earth and over every creeping*
> *thing that creeps on the earth." 27 So God cre-*
> *ated man in His own image; in the image of*
> *God He created him; male and female He cre-*
> *ated them."*

The emphasis here is on the plural pronouns used during the creation process; "Let US" implies there was a heavenly agreement in making man and what his assignment will be.

This Genesis Principle states that EVERYTHING THAT GOD CREATES AND IS ALIVE HAS TO OPERATE IN AGREEMENT WITH SOMETHING ELSE. This principle is so profound that God Himself has to operate by it. What He creates (*Bara*), He blessed (*Barak*). His creations work in harmony with one another, and when these conditions exist, great power is released.

One example of the Principle of Agreement found in the Bible is a familiar story called the Tower of Babel (Gen. 11).

Now the whole earth had <u>one language and one speech</u>. And it came to pass, as they journeyed from the east, that they found a plain in the land of Shinar, and they dwelt there. Then they said to one another, "Come, <u>let us</u> make bricks and bake them thoroughly." They had brick for stone, and they had asphalt for mortar. And they said, "Come, <u>let us</u> build ourselves a city, and a tower whose top is in the heavens; <u>let us</u> make a name for ourselves, <u>lest we</u> be scattered abroad over the face of the whole earth." But the Lord came down to see the city and the tower which the sons of men had built. And the Lord said, "Indeed the people are one and they all have one language, and this is what they begin to do; now nothing that they propose to do will be withheld from them. Come, <u>let Us</u> go down and there confuse their language, that they may not understand one another's speech." So the Lord scattered them abroad from there over the face of all the earth, and they ceased building the city. Therefore its name is called Babel, because there the Lord confused the language of all the earth; and from there the Lord scattered them abroad over the face of all the earth.

Imagine, Nimrod building a tower that had the potential to reach heaven! Because they were in agreement–one language and one speech, they all agreed to use bricks to build a city and a tower. God Himself confirmed that the people are operating in a principle that He created. The wording is powerful and one that hopefully every couple, supervisor, or pastor would employ: *"and this is what they begin to do; now nothing that they propose to do will be withheld from them."* Notice that God did not annihilate Nimrod for his efforts; He simply confounded their language, which disabled their ability to communicate or agree.

> (Acts 2:1-12). *"When the day of Pentecost came, they were all together in one place. Suddenly a sound like the blowing of a violent wind came from heaven and filled the whole house where they were sitting. They saw what seemed to be tongues of fire that separated and came to rest on each of them. All of them were filled with the Holy Spirit and began to speak in other tongues as the Spirit enabled them. Now there were staying in Jerusalem God fearing Jews from every nation under heaven. When they heard this sound, a crowd came together in bewilderment, because each one heard them speaking in his own language. Utterly amazed, they asked: "Are not all these men who are speaking Galileans? Then how is it that each of us hears them in his own native language? Parthians, Medes and Elamites; residents of Mesopotamia, Judea and Cappadocia, Pontus and Asia, Phrygia and Pamphylia, Egypt and the parts of Libya near Cyrene; visitors from Rome (both Jews and converts to Judaism); Cretans and Arabs — we hear them declaring the wonders of God in our own tongues!" Amazed*

*and perplexed, they asked one another, "What
does this mean?"*

The difference between Acts 2 and Genesis 11 is that
in Acts 2, the people were not trying to make a name for
themselves. The apostles and the others were too afraid
to step outside for fear of the Jews, but they prayed,
waited, expected, and anticipated the POWER AND THE
PROMISE OF THE HOLY GHOST. What was released
was something of biblical and historical proportions.

> *"A sound came from heaven like a rushing
> mighty wind and it filled the whole house where
> they were sitting and there appeared unto them
> cloven tongues of fire and it sat on each of them
> and they were ALL filled with the Holy Ghost
> and spoke with other tongues as the spirit gave
> them utterance".*

v.12 What meaneth this?

v.16 *This is THAT...* which was spoken by the
Prophet Joel...

Have you ever been to an Intercessory Prayer session
and someone starts praying, proclaiming, decreeing, and
declaring a thing when all of a sudden your spirit begins
to agree with what there are saying and a *"Yes," "Amen"*
comes out of you?

Tongues begin to flow; prophetic utterances take place.
You may not have even wanted to be there, but because
this divine principle has been activated your atmosphere
has shifted to encounter a powerful spiritual experience.

CAN I TALK TO THE CHURCH FOR A MINUTE? When the pastor makes a statement or has a vision for something, the whole church should set themselves in agreement with he or she sees...knowing that it is given to take the church further toward growth and community impact.

On a more personal note...

- Christians ought to be some of the most agreeable people on Earth
- You have to agree with yourself, in order to operate in EXCELLENCE.
- You have to agree with <u>yourself</u> (BODY – SOUL – SPIRIT). The reality of losing weight, living a healthy lifestyle, or even taking certain classes are great ideas, but they will remain as ideas, until you agree with yourself that change is necessary.
- Moms and Dads must agree (children can detect where there is no agreement)
- Husbands and wives must agree, in order for the relationship to last long.

I encourage every reader to find someone to get in agreement with or who will get in agreement with you. This will give you the opportunity to activate a principle that may be dormant in your or their lives. Agreement breeds life!

Romans 12:3 says, *"For I say, through the grace given unto me, to every man that is among you, not to think of himself more highly than he ought to think; but to think soberly, according as God hath dealt to every man the measure of faith."*

When you think about it, Faith, at its essence, is based on the Principle of Agreeing with God on matters that you cannot see with the natural eye-but on what God has spoken.

AGREEMENT CHANGES THE ATMOSPHERE
(Mark 9:14-29: Help thou my unbelief)

Albert Einstein: *"The significant problems we face cannot be solved from the same level that we created them, we must go up – in order to solve our problems."*

Three words: Atmosphere – Climate – Culture

This story is about a miracle that was preceded by the Principle of Agreement which shifted the power to heal to Christ's ability and not the man's. Once the <u>atmosphere</u> (mood) is set, the <u>climate</u> (the environment of the group) is shifted toward the whole <u>culture</u> and the pervading character of the whole church is shifted to believe God.

AGREEMENT CHANGES THE ATMOSPHERE.

You can change the atmosphere in your home, church, and city by what you agree with in the spirit. Three things to consider:

1. <u>Atmosphere</u>: A distinctive quality, as of a place; character, a surrounding or pervading mood, environment, or influence.)
2. <u>Climate</u>: The prevailing attitudes, standards, or environmental conditions of a group.)
3. <u>Culture:</u> Development or improvement of the mind by education or training, the behaviors and

beliefs characteristic of a particular social, ethnic, or age group: the youth culture; the drug culture.)

When you set the <u>atmosphere</u>, you set the <u>climate</u> or conditions for God's presence to be released and miracles to occur.

When you set the <u>climate</u>, you establish the <u>culture</u> (condition of the people) for the miracles to occur.

Question…what is the atmosphere like in your home, church, or work environment? Is there tension or is there joy?, Is there excitement and vitality or is it mundane? You can change it by establishing this Genesis Principle–remember God watches over his Word to perform it!

Agreement sets the atmosphere for FAITH AND MATURITY to be released.

The measure of the stature of the fullness of Christ is clearly seen when we look at these words in proper context.

THIS IS HOW THE ATMOSPHERE IN THE CHURCH SHIFTS THE POWER BACK TO GOD

Miracles, signs, and wonders should be a norm in the church. Deliverance, healings, and salvations occur in our services because we have people in our congregation who have set themselves in agreement that it is the Will of God for our church.

Worship sets the atmosphere for faith and maturity to be released, and God will open up heaven and pour out His blessings wherever there is an agreement with His Word.

2 Kings chapter 7, speaks of four men who had leprosy. Here they stand with a health condition that caused them to be outcast. This disease was so infectious that they called both the doctors and the priests. Why? 1)

Because there was no known cure and 2) because they weren't sure if it was a purely physical condition or a spiritual condition...Either way, if you had the condition...you had to leave!

There they sit on the mountainside and deliberate between themselves *(can you see them?)*. Let's eaves drop into their conversation.

> 2 Kings 7:3- "...*and they said one to another, Why sit we here until we die? If we say, We will enter into the city, then the famine is in the city, and we shall die there: and if we sit still here, we die also. Now therefore come, and let us fall unto the host of the Syrians: if they save us alive, we shall live; and if they kill us, we shall but die. And they rose up in the twilight, to go unto the camp of the Syrians: and when they were come to the uttermost part of the camp of Syria, behold, there was no man there. For the Lord had made the host of the Syrians to hear a noise of chariots, and a noise of horses, even the noise of a great host: and they said one to another, Lo, the king of Israel hath hired against us the kings of the Hittites, and the kings of the Egyptians, to come upon us. Wherefore they arose and fled in the twilight, and left their tents, and their horses, and their asses, even the camp as it was, and fled for their life. And when these lepers came to the uttermost part of the camp, they went into one tent, and did eat and drink, and carried thence silver, and gold, and raiment, and went and hid it; and*

*came again, and entered into another tent, and
carried thence also, and went and hid it".*

Here are the four lepers, outcasts from society, sat at
the gate of Samaria. Because of their disease, it is doubtful
anyone in the city cared what became of them. Like the
rest of Samaria during that time, these four men were
starving to death. Unlike the rest of Samaria, they decided
to do something about their situation.

The lepers began by asking the most important question: *"Why sit we here until we die?"*

Unfortunately, many people, families, and churches
never reach the point where they ask that question,
choosing instead to sit around and become complacent
about their discomfort and condition.

The lepers also realized they had just three options:
(just like many churches, families, marriages and
individuals):

A. Go back to the city and die (we can't go back)
B. Sit right there where they were and die (we can't
    stay here).
C. Go the camp of the enemy on the slim chance the
    Syrians would give them something to eat (in
    others words, go forward).

Of the three, only Option C offered any hope whatsoever. There was a better-than-average chance the Syrians
would kill them outright, but perhaps they would
have mercy.

So, at midnight (the darkest hour), the four lepers
took courage and began walking towards the camp of

Syria, a <u>place of uncertainty</u> and a <u>place of faith</u>. And as they went, God made their footsteps to sound like the Army of Israel. In fear, the Syrian soldiers left their tents, gold, silver, food, horses and clothes right there for these four lepers to take advantage. Ultimately, this miracle saved the city from famine. Notice, God didn't use the king or his cautious counselors; He used four societal outcasts (radicals) who were willing to face the facts, make a decision, and move forward in faith and agreement.

The scripture never says that they were healed; that's not the point. Instead it focuses on the greater issue, which was their agreement to move forward, which led to provisions for God's people.

At some point in life, we all face what appears to be "no-win situations"; I call it <u>Defining Moments</u>. It's where life, career or ministry forces you to make some changes in direction, habits or beliefs. Sometimes it seems every road leads to ruin. When we step out in faith, we open the door for God to work a miracle-which I define as "that which we cannot not do on our own."

Dictionary.com says, "Courage is the quality of mind or spirit that enables a person to face difficulty, change, danger, or pain without fear. It means to act in accordance with one's beliefs, especially in spite of criticism."

In this story, they did what every church, every family, every marriage, and every individual MUST do when faced (not with a physical disease) but with the debilitating diseases of apathy, or a "stuck in a rut" mentality. It's crippling to feel you just can't go forward, especially when you see others making progress.

Some miracles will never occur until there is some point of agreement reached. At its core, Faith means getting into agreement with what God says, even when you can't see all the details or have all the information.

ONE MORE STORY…In John 5:32, Jesus meets a man who had a health condition for thirty-eight years. There were a lot of people gathered at the Pool of Bethesda, people who were invalids, blind, lame, and paralyzed, waiting for the moving of the water. It was said that when an angel came and touched the water, whoever stepped in first was healed of WHATEVER diseases he had!

Jesus addressed one man in particular; Jesus saw him lying there and asked, "Do you want to be healed?" What a question to ask! What kind of question is that? A VERY VALID ONE! It is one that defines your moment. If you want, this disease lifted off you must get into agreement with what Jesus is presenting to you.

The man said to Jesus, *"Sir, I have no one to put me into the pool when the water is stirred. But while I am coming, another steps down before me.* Jesus said, "Rise, take up your bed and walk." There he sat at the Pool of Bethesda waiting, waiting, waiting for someone to help him to get in the pool. HOW LONG…have you been in this condition? THIRTY-EIGHT YEARS IS TOO LONG! I believe Jesus comes into a church or a person's life to declare…"Enough is enough"!

When faced with whether to go forward or not, many people, couples, churches, and families have chosen to simply wait for someone to do something or say something to help them. I come to you today to encourage you to take the courage to get going, just like those 4 lepers.

Ask any pastor, husband, or CEO how important agreement is to the relationships that surround them. You will discover God's principle in full effect, even if they don't acknowledge Him. The principle works whether you are Christian or not.

God Himself is a tri-part being: Father, Son, and Holy Ghost, and so are we-body, soul and spirit! Our greatest hindrances sometimes come from us not being in agreement with ourselves.

Consider the person who wants to stop a bad habit, lose weight, or progress in their career. If the desire and effort don't match, chances are that person will not attain their goal. There has to be a place of agreement within each of us to have the grit to win! When you do, the Principles of Agreement go into effect, and God watches over His Word to perform it.

IN THE WORKPLACE

Having a set of core beliefs sets a standard for agreement within an organization. They are the guiding principles that dictate behavior and can help people understand the difference between right and wrong. This sets parameters for agreement to achieve the goals of the organization. Great success can be achieved when all organizational leaders operate in the Spirit of Agreement.

When I worked in corporate America, I had several department supervisors under my authority. Even though they worked on different floors within the same building and some had different operation taskings, I would take my supervisors off site to discuss my personal objectives in helping them stay on the same accord. What resulted was a sense of synergy and creativity as the cross-talk and exchange of ideas that fostered momentum and increased productivity.

IN THE HOME

After thirty-nine years of marriage, I have discovered that when my wife and I are operating in the Principle of Agreement, we are unstoppable! I have also discovered that when we are not, we flounder. Amos 3:3 says, *"How can two walk together unless they agree?"* The "walking" here is synonymous with making progress.

Whether it is buying a home, making an investment, or committing to a healthy lifestyle, any progress is greatly enhanced when there is an agreement.

Regardless of how attractive an offer may be, I advise every couple to "agree as touching" before committing to anything, especially financial decisions.

WORDS WE LIVE BY

- EVERYTHING THAT GOD CREATES AND IS ALIVE HAS TO OPERATE IN AGREEMENT WITH SOMETHING ELSE.
- When the pastor makes a statement or has a vision for something, the whole church should set themselves in agreement with he or she sees… knowing that it given to take the church further toward growth and community impact.
- When you think about it, Faith… at its essence is based on the Principle of Agreeing with God on matters that you cannot see with the natural eye but on what God has spoken.
- Once the atmosphere (mood) is set, the climate (the environment of the group) is shifted toward

the whole culture, and the pervading character of the whole church is shifted to believe God.

- Defining Moments…It's where life, career, or ministry force you to make some changes in indirection, habits or beliefs.
- Whether it is buying a home, making an investment or committing to a healthy lifestyle, any progress is greatly enhanced when there is an agreement.

PRINCIPLE AND POWER OF REPRODUCTION

Genesis 1:11- *Then God said, "Let the earth bring forth grass, the herb that yields seed, and the fruit tree that yields fruit <u>according to its kind, whose seed is in itself,</u> on the earth"; and it was so. 12 And the earth brought forth grass, the herb that yields seed <u>according to its kind,</u> and the tree that yields fruit, <u>whose seed is in itself according to its kind.</u> And God saw that it was good.*

So God created great sea creatures and every living thing that moves, with which the waters abounded, <u>according to their kind,</u> and every winged bird according to its kind. And God saw that it was good. 22 And God blessed them, saying, "Be fruitful and multiply, and fill the waters in the seas, and let birds multiply on the earth." 23 So the evening and the morning were the fifth day.

24 Then God said, "Let the earth bring forth the living creature <u>according to its kind:</u> cattle and creeping thing and beast of the earth, each <u>according to its kind</u>"; and it was so. 25 And God made the beast of the earth <u>according to its

*kind, cattle according to its kind, and every-
thing that creeps on the earth according to its
kind.* **And God saw that it was good.**

The pattern in this Genesis Principle is clear; it is
"according to its kind." EVERYTHING THAT GOD
CREATED AND IS ALIVE reproduces *"after its own kind.*
This is God's plan for reproduction and posterity. Whether
it be trees, seed, birds, herbs, grass, families, churches, or
businesses, reproduction is essential to the continuance
of the species or relationship.

My favorite example of the principle is the seed. When
God created trees, He placed within the tree the ability
to create seeds. Within the seeds are more trees that also
have the ability to produce more seeds. This continuum is
a powerful example of how families, churches, businesses,
and relationships maintain their growth and existence

Any Darwinist would have issue with this statement,
but I assure you God did not create the modifications man
has created in order to help a species exist. Myles Munroe
taught us long ago in his book, *In Pursuit of Purpose "…
that when the purpose of a thing is not clear, abuse of that thing
is inevitable."*

In other words, man can modify what God has created and can use it for good or bad. Let's say God created
a plant with the medical ability inside of it to cure pain.
Man can take that same plant and abuse it as a narcotic
to make lots of money.

Jesus presents a perfect example of the Principle and
Power of Reproduction. Look at some of His statements
in the Bible regarding his relationship with the Father…

- (John 10:30) He said, "My Father and I are One"
- (John 5:17) "My Father works, hitherto I work"
- (John 5:19) "The Son can do nothing of himself, but that what he sees the Father doing, for what things He doeth these thigs also doeth the Son likewise."
- (John 5:23) "He that honors the Father should likewise honor the Son."
- (John 5:26,27) "For as the Father has life in himself, so hath he given to the Son to have life in himself and hath given him authority to execute judgment, because he is the Son of man."
- John 8:42 "For I proceeded forth and came from God, neither came I of myself, but He sent me"

The apostle Paul put it best in I Corinthians 11:1 when he said, "*Follow me as I follow Christ.*"

Need I go on?

My pastor, the late Bishop Nate Holcomb, shared a powerful insight with many churches and pastors coming under his Covenant Connections International (CCI) umbrella called "*Baptized in the Franchise.*" He taught us that just as you can cannot buy a "whopper" at McDonalds, nor can you buy a Big Mac at Burger King, churches under CCI should do as those successful franchises have done–Follow the pattern.

Copying the latest church fad or most popular preacher may not give you that success you are searching for. He was essentially telling us, "I am reproducing myself in YOU". The sustained success of thirty-nine years of ministry with hundreds of churches underneath him nationally and internationally serves as an excellent example of "how to do ministry the RIGHT way."

Reproduction is why mentorship and coaching is becoming more and more popular these days. Showing younger ones or inexperienced ones how to do marriage, ministry, career, or educational pursuits helps them receive valuable knowledge that will pay huge dividends latter on in life.

In Divine Relationships, I believe God orchestrates people to come into your life to bless you by pouring a little of themselves into you. The only caveat here is to take the characteristics and qualities of certain individuals that are positive, healthy, and pertinent to your own benefit. I have had many people who wanted to speak into my life. My first question is "Are they living what they are sharing with me?" In other words, if their advice doesn't line up with their lifestyle, I question its validity.

IN THE HOME

When I lived in Brooklyn, New York, as a teenager, we were mentored by a man named Jimmy Mitchell. He coached us, taught us valuable life lessons like how to survive in the streets, stand up to let a lady sit down if you are riding the city bus or the train…he reproduced himself in us. As I got older, I carried these same behaviors everywhere I traveled around the world.

As a pastor, I try to reproduce myself in church leaders in our church. It is so much easier to accomplish church growth and stability when leaders have and operate in the same earnest care, same spirit of faith, same love and show the same diligence as I do regarding the work of the ministry.

I try to reproduce my heart and concerns in every aspect of church ministry and operations. It reminds me of Ephesians 4:12 which talks about, "...*perfecting the saints for the work of the ministry and the edifying the body of Christ...*" I use this scripture often when getting church members involved with community projects and activities. I have discovered that there is usually a spiritual dimension to every work, which could cause people to get frustrated or offended if they don't have the heart of the pastor or church leaders.

Philippians 2:5 says, *Let this mind be in you, which was also in Christ Jesus.* This has become a divine strategy in dealing with people, production, and processes that pertain to church and ministry activities; for me, the old adage *What Would Jesus Do* is as relevant today as it was when first spread out in the early '90's.

IN THE WORKPLACE

In the workplace, mentorship and internship is invaluable to the development of a person's career path. Any young ambitious college grads can be impressionable and will do whatever is asked of them. When I worked in management, I never placed the younger ones under overbearing, bossy, and highly aggressive and money-hungry people. I placed them under people who had a well-balanced perspective of the company and their family.

Anybody can tell you how to climb the ladder of success, but I sought out people who are where I wanted to be, doing what I wanted to do and living the style I wanted to live...and then I copied it (with my own slight modifications). I agree, *imitation is the highest form of flattery or compliment.*

WORDS WE LIVE BY

- EVERYTHING THAT GOD CREATED AND IS ALIVE, REPRODUCES "AFTER ITS OWN KIND." This is God's plan for reproduction and posterity
- Within the seeds are more trees that also have the ability to produce more seeds. This continuum is a powerful example of how families, churches, businesses, and relationships maintain their growth and existence.
- When God created trees, He placed within the tree the ability to create seeds.
- Reproduction is why mentorship and coaching is becoming more and more popular these days. Showing younger ones or inexperienced ones how to do marriage, career, or educational pursuits helps them receive valuable knowledge that will pay huge dividends latter on in life.
- Anybody can tell you how to climb the ladder of success. But I seek people who are where I want to be, doing what I what to do in life and living the style I want to live...and then I copy it (with my own slight modifications).

PRINCIPLE & POWER OF RESPIRATION

———— ✳ ————

The Principle of Respiration says this…EVERYTHING THAT GOD CREATED AND IS ALIVE HAS TO BREATHE (people, plants, fish, trees, relationships, churches, families, businesses). Humans breathe in oxygen and breathe out carbon dioxide; plants breathe in carbon dioxide and breathe out the very oxygen that we need to breathe in - a perfect balance. Breathing is a means by which we stay alive–this is God's design for sustaining and maintaining life.

Genesis 2:7 says, *"And the LORD God formed man of the dust of the ground, and breathed into his nostrils the breath of life* (which is the essence of life); *and man became a living* (Heb: *chay* = flowing, alive, revived) *soul* (a creature, person, appetite, mind, living being, desire, emotion, passion, a living being with life in its blood).

Finally, Adam is born! He is created in the likeness of God. Eden is now a stable environment for Adam to exist and accomplish his purpose (be fruitful, multiply, take dominion and give stuff a name!) God waters the ground, and forms man from the dust of the earth and there stands Adam as a lifeless shell of a man who resembles God, can you see him?

Then God does something incredible: He *"breathed into his nostrils the Breath of Life and man (Adam) became a living soul."*

Most men's conferences that I have been to (*Total Men's Fellowship, PromiseKeepers, Manpower*) are opportunities for men to get back in balance (just like breathing). Many men are so asphyxiated (lose consciousness by impaired breathing) by the daily pressures of life that their wives send them and pray that someone will breathe the breath of life (resuscitate) back into them so the man can, in turn, breathe into the family again.

Many marriages are fragmented because nobody is breathing life into the marriage.

1. Not devotional or prayer
2. No leading home Bible study
3. No prophetic utterances over their family.

So no wonder why so many wives are frustrated, disillusioned and hard to get along with! They are frustrated because if no one freely breathes, invests or sows into her words; cast vision;, or displays leadership–she is disabled from her God-given characteristics to be a *"Help meet,"* to reproduce, nurture, buy, or reflect that which is sown into her.

We had a couple in my church several years ago where the husband would get mad at me because when he would tell his wife something, she wouldn't do it, then I would say the <u>same thing</u> across the pulpit during the message and she would say, "Babe, let's do such a thing, because Pastor says...."

When a pastor receives the inspired Word of God, and he speaks (breathes) that same Word over the men and women in the audience who are in relationships that have lost their consciousness or life–it resuscitates or revives and brings them back to life.

When men breathe life into their families, churches and others there can be a balance. However, sometimes the pressures of life make it difficult to sort things out – we come to the end of our rope and we don't know what to do, we can't breathe on our own, so we need artificial respiration (someone to breathe into us).

I learned CPR when I was in the Air Force. It is a life-saving technique whose purpose is to maintain the flow of oxygenated blood to the brain and the heart, thereby delaying tissue death (which is often irreversible). After a few minutes, brain cells die and cannot be reversed. If you see someone in that state, it is far better to do something than do nothing at all.

This is what happens when we go to church, Bible study or take classes. The Man (or Woman) of God speaks LIFE. When you receive with meekness the engrafted word, it will restore your soul (consciousness). That's why you feel revived when the preacher preaches, teaches or exhorts.

Prayer, worship, and preaching are forms of breathing. Counsel is a way another form of breathing. The lyrics of Michael W. Smith song, "Breathe" hold true, which says, *"This is the air I breathe,…Your Holy presence living in me… and I am lost without you"*, Israel Houghton wrote… *So breathe into me once again.*

Breathing (respiration) is a way of exchange. You cannot just breathe <u>in</u> only; you have to breathe <u>out</u> as well. That's too simple isn't it? This exchange is God's design for sustaining life. It's a vital sign that doctors use to determine the health of a patient. If this is true in the natural, isn't it quite true in the spirit realm?

Consider the following scripture passage, it's an incredible story.

Ezekiel 37:1-14 (MSG)

> *God grabbed me. God's Spirit took me up and set me down in the middle of an open plain strewn with bones. He led me around and among them — a lot of bones! There were bones all over the plain — dry bones, bleached by the sun. He said to me, "Son of man, can these bones live?" I said, "Master God, only you know that." He said to me, "Prophesy over these bones: 'Dry bones, listen to the Message of God!'" God, the Master, told the dry bones, "Watch this: I'm bringing the breath of life to you and you'll come to life. I'll attach sinews to you, put meat on your bones, cover you with skin, and breathe life into you. You'll come alive and you'll realize that I am God!" I prophesied just as I'd been commanded (here is obedience). As I prophesied, there was a sound and, oh, rustling! The bones moved and came together, bone to bone. I kept watching. Sinews (tendons) formed, then muscles on the bones, then skin stretched over them. But they had no breath in them. He said to me, "Prophesy to the breath. Prophesy, son of man. Tell the breath, 'God, the Master, says, Come from the four winds. Come, breath. Breathe on these slain bodies. Breathe life!'" So I prophesied, just as he commanded me. The*

*breath entered them and they came alive! They
stood up on their feet, a huge army. Then God
said to me, "Son of man, these bones are the
whole house of Israel. Listen to what they're
saying: 1)'Our bones are dried up, 2) our hope
is gone,3) there's nothing left of us.' "Therefore,
prophesy. Tell them, 'God, the Master, says: I'll
dig up your graves and bring you out alive – O
my people! Then I'll take you straight to the
land of Israel. When I dig up graves and bring
you out as my people, you'll realize that I am
God. I'll breathe my life into you and you'll live.
Then I'll lead you straight back to your land and
you'll realize that I am God. I've said it and I'll
do it. God's Decree.*

When men breathe, life comes forth!

When men breathe, there is a sense of freedom.

When men breathe, the atmosphere is charged for praise and worship.

When men breathe, hope is restored, joy is manifested.

When men breathe, balance of life is restored.

Some relationships are on life support or artificial respiration because men are not breathing into their families. They need someone to breathe into them-we all do! Christian cable networks like TBN, INSP, and WORD do a good job in presenting great preachers and teachers. However, none of these networks can do what YOU are designed to do. No wonder there are so many frustrated people and misguided youths in our society.

Sons and daughters need a father figure to breathe into them.

Brothers and sisters need other brothers and sisters to breathe into them

Fathers need to breathe into their sons and daughters, even if they are not yours biologically.

Pastors need other pastors and ministers to breathe into them. WHY? Because pastors <u>have to</u> breathe life into their congregation. And congregations have to breathe into the pastor. It's the Principle of Exchange all over again!

In John 6:63, Jesus said, *"It is the spirit that quickeneth; the flesh profiteth nothing: the words that I speak unto you, they are spirit, and they are life."*

One last example… John 20:22 "Again he said, *"Peace be with you. As the Father has sent me, so I am sending you."* Then he breathed on them and said, *"Receive the Holy Spirit."*.

It is one of Jesus" last acts of impartation. Jesus knew what we should know, the church cannot stand on the strength and intelligence of men nor the arm of our flesh. There is not enough life in them to sustain the awesome task of restoration of God's people. They will need something more, something supernatural –hey need the Holy Ghost, the Spirit of Life itself dwelling inside them.

Can I be honest? Sometimes, all I need is one Word from the Lord in order to bring me back to life. Even when I mess up, I need God to breathe into me words of life and encouragement. What He says may cut me to the core, but whatever You do Lord, don't stop breathing into me! Your words are spirit and they are life, and I need it desperately.

A person can get shot, stabbed, or cut, disease can come and try to wipe them out, but as long as they are breathing–they still have a chance! No one can pronounce you as dead as long as you are still breathing!

ONE MORE POINT...A pastor friend of mine from Virginia gave an analogy that left an indelible image in my mind. He said the boa constrictor's killing technique is a reminder of how the pressures of life can squeeze out the life of any of us. He said when the boa strikes its victim, it releases just enough venom to anesthetize its prey. Once it gets woozy and somewhat paralyzed, the boa then coils itself around the victim and every time it breathes, the boa squeezes tighter, crushing bones and organs in the process. Bones represent the infrastructure of a person, and when those bones are crushed, the boa has the audacity to flit its tongue to see if the victim is still breathing. If it is, the boa continues to squeeze until there is no more life in the victim. Then, it un-hinges its jaw and approaches the victim face first and consumes the victim–whole.

This graphic illustration showed me that life can sting you with setbacks and disappointments; life will try to squeeze the very life out of any of us. It constricts my time with the Lord, my family and my health; breaks my faith and attempt to consume my dreams, vision, and purpose.

I pray after reading this section, you will take a moment to pray and reclaim everything that has been stolen from you through the busyness of life!

WORDS WE LIVE BY

- The Principle of Respiration says this... EVERYTHING THAT GOD CREATED AND IS ALIVE HAS TO BREATHE.

- Breathing is a means by which we stay alive–this is God's design for sustaining and maintaining life.

- Many people are so asphyxiated (lose consciousness by impaired breathing) by the daily pressures of life that their wives send them and pray that someone will breathe the breath of life (resuscitate) back into them so the man can, in turn, breathe into the family again.

- When a pastor receives the inspired Word of God, and he speaks (breathes) that same Word over the men and women in the audience who are in relationships that have lost their consciousness or life–it resuscitates or revives and brings them back to life.

- Sometimes all I need is one Word from the Lord in order to bring me back to life. Even when I mess up, I need God to breathe into me. What He says may cut me to the core, but whatever You do Lord, don't stop breathing into me!

- The busyness of life will try to squeeze the very joys of life out of any of us. It constricts my time with the Lord, my family and my health; it will break my faith; and attempt to consume my dreams, vision, and purpose.

PRINCIPLE & POWER OF SEED TIME & HARVEST

G enesis 8:22 *"While the earth remains, seed time and har-vest, and cold and heat, and summer and winter, and day and night shall not cease."*

Genesis 1:14 says *"…divide the day from the night; and let them be for <u>signs and seasons</u>, and for days and years."*

This principle says that EVERYTHING THAT GOD CREATES AND IS ALIVE OPERATES AND GROWS BY WAY OF <u>SEASONS</u>. When I first started pastoring I used to think that Seed Time and Harvest was only about money–I was wrong! During the creation process God established a dynamic called *Seasons*.

Growing up in Brooklyn, New York, the only thing I knew about seasons was Winter, Spring, Summer, and Fall, then when we moved to San Angelo, Texas, we were made more aware of the agricultural aspects of seasons, sowing, harvest, threshing, and plowing seasons because we now live in a rural community.

I saved this one for last because it speaks to so many dynamics in life. I have preached, taught, and lectured on this subject numerous times and it is near and dear to my heart. I will apologize ahead of time if I digress, but there is so much in me regarding this principle.

The Principle of Seed Time and Harvest relates to all of the ones previously addressed, but is not limited to them. Only God orchestrates the times and seasons of a persons' life. In Acts 1:7, we find this interesting insight:

> "When they (the disciples) therefore were come together, they asked of him, saying, *Lord, wilt thou at* <u>*this time*</u> *restore again the kingdom to Israel?* And he said unto them, *It is not for you to know the times or the seasons, which the Father hath put in his own power*".

Jesus is letting them know that what happened under the *Davidic Covenant* may not happen as expected when He departs; as matter of fact, don't concern yourselves with the "when's" of life.

However, their question is a valid one! It is not for you to know the times or the seasons, which the Father hath put in his own power. Essentially, they are asking Jesus...

1. When You depart, surely You're not going to leave things in the hands of the chief priests and rulers again, are You?

2. Surely the Kingdom of Israel (old order) would be placed in power again as in the days of David and Solomon, won't it?

My Two Definitions for Time:

1. *Chronos*

- A space of time which designates a fixed or special occasion
- A particular time or interval (minute, hour, day, month, year, etc.)

2. *Kairos* (season)

- One of four divisions of the year–winter, spring, summer, fall
- A recurring period marked by certain activities, celebrations, or crops
- A natural or convenient time
- To enhance the flavor of food by adding something to it.

When something is IN SEASON, that means it is legally available, it is the right time or proper moment. (getting out of debt in season now)

When something is OUT OF SEASON that means it is out of cycle, not the right time. (A word spoken out of season marks that person to be a fool)

My Rules of Engagement concerning SEASONS are simple:

1. Don't skip seasons of life (son, brother, husband, and father).
2. When a season comes, it brings with it the requirement to change.
3. The season you are in prepares you for your next season.
4. Just as no one can change the season naturally, neither can we change the season; only God can do that!
5. You will know when the season is changing because their will come feelings of anxiety, anticipation, expectation and discomfort.

When change threatens your comfort zone don't make the mistake like many people, by retreating to a place of excuses, procrastination and defeatism.

One of the unique things about living in San Angelo is how quickly the weather can change. It is a common phrase in our town that says, *"If you don't like the weather, stick around for a minute–it'll change."*

Autumn is my favorite season. It requires constant change. It gets hot, then cools down, then a little rain here and there. It is VERY inconvenient. I asked my church recently, *"Did you catch the change in season? It was very smooth, wasn't it? First it rained, then it got cool ...and before you knew it...the shift occurred. Have you noticed... leaves are falling off of trees, it is cooler in the mornings, getting darker earlier, not as many fire ants?* Summer was over.

Just as we were starting to see a change in the weather, I also saw a change (a shift) in the spiritual realm in our church. New families were being added to the church as unreliable and inconsistent members were leaving.

If it were up to us, there would only be Spring or Summer seasons. We like things rosy and warm. But understanding the <u>purpose of a season</u> is vitality important for your spiritual and personal development.. for you, your family, and your church!

God will change things in the atmosphere before you see it manifested in your life. Isaiah 43:18 says *"Behold, I do a new thing, Shall ye not see it?"* All we need to do is to look up, and we will see the atmospheric changes (shifts in the spirit realm) that would tell us "Get ready...a Change is coming". God does NOT have to wait until September 22 to bring in the Fall Season.

Have you ever sensed strange things happening in the atmosphere that you could not define?

I used to laugh at my auntie because she used to be able to tell when it was going to rain because her joints started to act funny. I discovered that barometric pressure in the atmosphere affects our joints, so it was not just an old wives tales. Some people can smell rain before one drop falls to the ground.

The human life has seasons much as the earth has seasons;, each season comes with its own particular beauty and power, blessings and challenges, and opportunities. By focusing on springtime and summer, we miss what God is calling *"The New Thing,"* which is a process of celebration and appreciation. Life is neither linear nor stagnant. It is movement from mystery to mystery, from faith to faith.

FIRST THE NATURAL, THEN THE SPIRITUAL

Seasons come to sustain life and balance. Our ecology is based on the changing seasons: plants, sea life, birds, horticulture, even people need the seasons of change.

It is bigger than you and I...so don't worry, ITS NOT YOUR FAULT THAT THE SEASONS ARE CHANGING. Trees and grass need Winter, butterflies need the Spring. The guy who takes care of our trees and shrubs often gives spiritual insights from a horticultural perspective. He doesn't know it, but he provides great sermon material because of his knowledge of how plants grow..I relate it to relationships.

There was a change that God was orchestrating with our Praise Team... we changed from strictly black ospel to more praise and worship, and surprisingly people from different backgrounds started attending our services. I told my church "Many of you are just ONE PRAISE AWAY from your breakthrough!" And just as we are going to have to make adjustments in clothing and schedules, we should also make changes spiritually.

Seasons of Change can sneak up on you if you are not watching with a sense of expectancy. With it comes blessings and challenges AT THE SAME TIME! If you don't take advantage of your Season of Change, you will become a victim of the Change.

WORDS WE LIVE BY

This principle says that EVERYTHING THAT GOD CREATES AND IS ALIVE operates and grows by way of seasons.

The Bible is a book about relationships only God orchestrates the times and seasons of a person's life.

When something is IN SEASON that means it is legally available, it is the right time or proper moment. (getting out of debt in season now) Glory!

When something is OUT OF SEASON that means it is out of cycle, not the right time. (a word spoken out of season marks that person to be a fool).

Don't skip seasons of life (son, brother, husband, and father).

When a season comes, it brings with it the requirement to change.

The season you are in prepares you for your next season

You will know when the season is changing because their will come feelings of anxiety, anticipation, expectation, and discomfort. The human life has seasons much as the earth has seasons; each season comes with its own particular beauty and power, blessings, challenges, and opportunities

SECTION IV

PURPOSE OF A SEASON

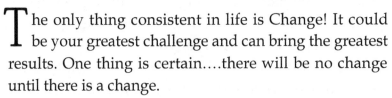

The only thing consistent in life is Change! It could be your greatest challenge and can bring the greatest results. One thing is certain....there will be no change until there is a change.

For some of the readers, I pray that this is your season to grow closer to the Lord; for others, it may be your season to make personal changes. The bottom line is... DON'T MISS YOUR SEASON!

Changes and seasons are various and pretty obvious.

Human development changes include: infant, child, adolescence, teens, young adult, career, mid-life, pre-retirement, retirement, and post-retirement.

Spiritual development changes include: salvation, loving God, loving others, serving God, serving others, following God, leading others, and reproducing yourself in others.

Marital development changes include (but not limited to): Seasons of Passion (called the Romance Stage), Parenting season, Settling Down season, Midlife season, and of course, the Second Half of Life season, which includes empty-nest syndrome, and all the other aspects of maintaining a healthy and happy marriage as a couple grows older together.

There are lots of books and references for this particular type of development; the point here is that even healthy marriages go through seasonal changes.

I told one of my sons when he was going through a difficult season in his young adult life, "It is time now to walk in the season of grace God has provided. Like in the game of chess-It's your move now to redeem your time, and make the personal changes in your life toward the perfect will of God. I told him…**God has to prepare you for what He has prepared for you!**

I love the words "Shift", "Transition", "Move", and "Stir." All are progressive words that indicate "Change." Here are a few nuggets of truth regarding seasons that I hope will be a blessing to you.

1. SEASONS BRING HOPE. It gives you something to look forward to. Physically, spiritually, emotionally, family, personal, or in the church; when a new season comes, it is filled with possibility and hope.
2. SEASONS BRING CHANGE. Genesis 1:14 says, *"Let the firmament of the heaven to divide the day from the night; and let them be for signs, and for seasons, and for days, and years."*

I believe that you will either embrace your Season of Change or you will become a victim of the season of change. Either way, God will be glorified.

Spiritually speaking. The purpose of our seasons is primarily to restore right relationship with our Father and continue the furtherance of your life! Along with that right relationship comes the prosperity, promises, protection, provisions, prophetic, peace, and the power. There is no need for boasting or bragging–you don't even need to tell anybody that you are in your season – they will know!

Consider this story about Mary and Joseph (Luke 2:49-52). They had to recede into the background as their Son took center stage in the drama of redemption. He whom they once called SON, they would later have to call "LORD." They knew their roles and embraced it.

3. SEASONS CANNOT BE STOPPED BY YOU. The power that controls a season is beyond our comprehension and defies our logic. Proverbs 19:21 says, *"Many are the plans in a man's heart, but it is the Lord's purpose that prevails."* The beginning and the ending of a season are not determined by man but by God's sovereign agenda.
4. SEASONS COME WITHOUT PERMISSION. God does not need your permission and will not ask you for the timing of a changing season. The arrival or change of a season does not need our blessing; it contains its own!

Hebrews 12:2... "Looking unto Jesus the AUTHOR AND FINISHER of our faith." He writes the scripts for our lives called SEASON 2020 (or whatever year your season of change occurs).

5. SEASONS BRING CHANGES THAT YOU CANNOT CONTROL. The heat of a summer in Texas, the cold winter in West Texas–no matter what our personal desire, wishes or attitudes may be, only God controls the seasons.

There are two players of the providential changes of seasons of life.

A. Those <u>to whom</u> the change is happening. Some like only Summer months and refuse to change. You can be the blessed recipient of change, like getting a new job or promotion.

B. Those <u>through whom</u> the change is happening. Believe it or not, you can make a difference in someone else's life! I teach people that we are blessed to be a blessing!

The choice is up to you! You can facilitate changes in your life and the lives of others by changing what you think, say, and do.

Consider 2 Kings 4:9-13 The story of the Shunamite Woman goes like this:

> *"...And she said unto her husband, Behold now, I perceive that this is a holy man of God, which passes by us continually. Let us make a little chamber, I pray thee, on the wall; and let us set for him there a bed, and a table, and a stool, and a candlestick: and it shall be, when he cometh to us, that he shall turn in thither. And it fell on a day, that he came thither, and he turned into the chamber, and lay there. And he said to Gehazi his servant, Call this Shunammite. And when he had called her, she stood before him. And he said unto him, Say now unto her,* **Behold, thou hast been careful for us with all this care; what is to be done for thee?***

Toward the end of this story, she reveals that a well-kept, deep-seated desire of her heart was to have a son.

Elisha spoke a prophetic word into her life. And he said, *"About this season, <u>according to the time of life</u>, thou shalt embrace a son. And she said, Nay, my lord, thou man of God, do not lie unto thine handmaid."*

There are some deep-seated dreams and desires in all of us that have not manifested yet. When we see someone else doing it, living in it, married to it or receiving it– we get shaken because of the possibility of that desire becoming a reality – especially if we have given up on the notion.

And the woman conceived, and bare a son at that season that Elisha had said unto her, according to the time of life. Because *she and her husband sowed into Elisha's life with a table, a bed and a candlestick, they got a blessing beyond understanding – a son was born!*

7. DON'T DENY THAT CHANGE IS HAPPENING. (John 9:1-11) When change is occurring in your life, seek to understand what is happening and accept its realities and commit to fulfilling the newness it demands of your life. Rationalizing that nothing is going on doesn't help you. Resistance is futile.

8. ADMIT THAT CHANGE IS NECESSARY. For some of you it is mandatory! In John 3:1-5, Nicodemus wanted a change, but because he was a High Priest, he couldn't let everyone know that he was secretly believing in Jesus. He approached Jesus by night to admit… he needed a change!

9. DON'T BE ANGRY WITH THE WAY CHANGE IS COMING. (Naaman–2 Kings 5:10,11). Nothing is more damaging to a developing relationship than an angry spirit. It produces emotionalism,

egotism and leads to sel –destructive decisions. Being angry with God is senseless. Change will make you uncomfortable but it is necessary.

10. DON'T BE PASSIVE OR IDLE. Never approach your season of change in a nonchalant, non-participative manner. Many people hesitate to embrace their season of change for their own personal reasons. This is defeatist. Windows of opportunities are like windows; they open and close sometimes quickly. Has procrastination caused you to miss blessed opportunities or relationships? I believe at the core of procrastination is fear.

11. SEASONS DO NOT GUARANTEE SUCCESS; they simply guarantee change. That's too simple, isn't it? The reality of this statement is that success in your season of change requires your involvement, passion, and commitment. With the change of season comes opportunities, blessings, and challenges that, I believe, point you in a direction to fulfill your *Life Assignment.*

12. DON'T BE TOO BUSY for God to change you. Remember when Jesus visited the home of Mary and Martha? Martha was so incumbered with care of household chores that she got angry with Jesus for not telling her sister Mary to help her (Luke 10:38-42). She was so busy with caring for their house that she could not sit at Jesus's feet like Mary.

13. DON'T BE UNPREPARED or caught off guard when your season of change occurs, In Exodus 12:11, Moses instructed families to eat their Passover meal with staff in hand and shoes on

their feet and eat quickly. God always demands preparation for impending change.

14. DON'T BOAST IN YOUR SEASON. When your season of change comes, there is no need to brag about it. People around you will recognize that something new and different is happening in your life. Matthew 5:16 says, *"Let your light so shine before men that they may see your good works and glorify the Father which is in heaven."*

TRANSITIONS THAT LEADS TO TRANSFORMATION

Everything that is ALIVE undergoes transition and transformation, just as individuals within the relationship changes.

Types of transformation include (but are not limited to): Spiritual, financial, physical, locational and emotional. There are no bragging rights if you are just transitioning without a transformation taking place. (example: marital engagement).

According to Dictionary.com Transition is: "The process of change: a process or period in which something undergoes a change and passes from one state, stage, form, or activity to another".

Transformation is: "The result of a change or alteration, especially a radical one, a change in position or direction."

TRANSITION is the Process, TRANSFORMATION is the Result of the Process. God is much more concerned about your Transformation than He is with your Transitions.

Couples, churches, and businesses who are afraid to transform and change, limit the potential of their success. The Bible is full of stories about people who made transitions–some good, some not so good. We ought to use these stories as a stepping stone to fulfill our purpose.

As I said before, the most important steps in life involve a PROCESS and you have to be willing to go through the paces and face the challenges that comes with your next opportunity. That is, if you want it bad enough!

I believe that until the frustration of where you are exceeds the challenge of moving forward, you will not go anywhere. In other words, if you are not frustrated with your weight, living situation, or job status, you are not likely to do something to facilitate a change. Even if that change is going to hurt a little or require a sacrifice, it is necessary to position you to advance.

We had a few Nigerian college students in our church a few years ago. Some of them were taking an incredible eighteen to twenty hours per semester. One student in particular was a 17 year old young lady who was very dedicated to her education. As compared to some of her young American colleagues, she was considered a nerd and lacking a social life. I asked her why she was so dedicated. She informed me that her US citizenship was based on her academic performance, her words were, "*I can't afford to fail, otherwise I risk being deported back to a poverty-ridden, highly criminalized environment in Lagos*".

As your family, career, business or church grows and prepares to make a move upward, onward, and outward, the people involved must also prepare to make a move upward. Additionally, the way you function, the character you demonstrate, and the way you communicate... none of these happen overnight–it is part of your transition to a closer walk with Christ and a deeper commitment to service. Anytime you attempt to do something big for God, you will be challenged to go through a phase of transition.

REVELATION FROM A 1960'S SITCOM

In the 1960's, there was a sitcom called The Beverly Hillbillies. The opening scene told the basic story of the show through its opening song; here are the lyrics... but you probably already know it.

> *Let me tell about a man named Jed, a poor mountaineer, barely kept his family fed when one day he was shootin' for some food, when up from the ground came a bubbling crude, black oil, Texas tea. Well the first thing you know ole Jed's a millionaire, Kin folks said, Jed... Move away from here Californy is the place you ought to be so they loaded up the truck and the moved to Beverly (Beverly Hills, California).*

There is so much to this theme song that relates to what I want to express in this section of the book. Once Jed became a millionaire, his kinfolks said, "Jed you <u>must</u> relocate." WHY? Because most millionaires don't live in the back hills of Tennessee, eating possum soup and drinking whiskey.

The funniest part of the show is to see HOW their transition and their transformation did not match! When they moved to California, they moved into a huge mansion that had a swimming pool which they called a "cement pond", and a pool table, which they called "*the fancy eatin' table*".

Even though they transitioned from the back hills country to a luxurious mansion in Beverly Hills, they never transformed in their mind and behavior.

Romans 12:2 says, "*...be ye transformed by the renewing of your mind that you may prove the perfect and acceptable will of God.*"

When I ministered this example recently, most people over age forty were laughing hysterically as they finished the words of the song along with me. They knew where I was going, without me having to complete my expressed thoughts on the subject. What was funny back then is as much of a reality to any of us who refused to transform to a new standard of living today.

I repeat...God is much more interested in your TRANSFORMATION than He is in transitioning you from one place or experience to another.

Every Christian has a testimony and every testimony involves a <u>process</u>. In order to live a victorious life we MUST complete each phase of our processes with integrity, character, grace, and style. Style? *Yes!* I teach leaders to go through their challenges with their heads held high, a positive confession, and looking good!

It's like the three Hebrews boy who were thrown into a fiery furnace (Daniel 3:27 NLT):

> *Then the high officers, officials, governors, and advisers crowded around them and saw that the fire had not touched them. Not a hair on their heads was singed, and their clothing was not scorched. They didn't even smell of smoke!*

To cheat or circumvent your challenges, tests, and trials is to cheat yourself out of the validity and credibility of your testimony when you come through it.

There are no bragging rights given to those who run away from every fight, dodge every confrontation and give themselves excuses as to why they can't finish what they start. Life is not a sprint–it's a marathon, it involves enduring to the end.

The processes of life are intricate, and the bigger the expected result, the more important every step of the process becomes. God sits on the throne of our lives "working all things out after the counsel of his own will (Eph. 1:11), "All things work together for good to those who love the Lord and to those who are called according to His purpose (Rom. 8:28).

Ephesians 1 says, *"He makes known unto us the mystery of His will, according to his good pleasure which He has purposed in himself"*.

In this case *(and there are plenty more in the Bible)*, a son was born *"according to the time of life."* When God does stuff like this, there is not a force on earth that can prevent it from happening.

By a certain age or stage in life, all of us should have given birth to something, have some great idea, do something that will propel you into your destiny. The God of Divine Relationships wants you to NEVER give up on what He has placed on the *Life Assignment* He has placed inside of you!

LIFE ASSIGNMENTS

———— ✳ ————

When I was in the military, you could get on the computer and choose bases which you wanted to be your next duty station. If you were lucky, you got your Base of Preference. Then one day, you received your assignment papers. If you were a first term airman, you had the grace to turn down an assignment if you didn't like it and wait for another to come your way. However, once you became a second-term or career airman, that grace was no longer available for you. If you declined an assignment, your next decision was to stay where you are or get out of the military.

The Bible says that Jesus is the "author and finisher of our faith" (Heb. 2:1). Here are some scriptures that helped us settle into San Angelo when the USAF assigned us here back in the mid-80's.

Revelation 1:8 says, "*I AM the Alpha and the Omega, the beginning and the end... which was, and which is to come, the Almighty.*

Isaiah 46:10 says, "*I am God, and there is none like me... Declaring the end from the beginning, and from ancient times the things that are not yet done, saying, My counsel shall stand, and I will do all my pleasure*

Romans 8:28 "*...and we know that ALL things work together for good to them that love God, to them who are called according to HIS purposes*".

When I take these scriptures into consideration, I believe all of us have a Life Assignment given by God to bless your life. It is in direct line with your purpose and destiny. I also believe that when you accept your *Life Assignment*, things, people, and resources strangely begin to line up.

I know people who lives frustrated lives because they did not accept their assignment and in doing so, made poor life decisions. They got involved with short cuts instead of working hard, some got involved with the wrong people because they thought someone else could fulfill their assignment.

It is heart-breaking to see young ones trying to catch up on the years poor decisions have wasted. So, in terms of Divine Relationships, here are a few Rules of Engagement regarding *Life Assignments*...

1. You do not pick your "life assignments" (destiny) GOD DOES!
2. Every life assignment is what you make of it
3. The timing of your next assignment may come when you least expect it
4. Assignments are given to meet a greater need—not just yours!
5. Your success at your present assignment can qualify you for your next assignment
6. There is an expectation for you to perform, NOT JUST SHOW UP!
7. At your next assignment, someone is waiting for you!

HOW TO APPROACH YOUR NEXT LIFE ASSIGNMENT

Change what you <u>say</u>, change what you <u>do</u>, change what you <u>think</u> and change your <u>associations</u>

Change What You Say. What you say about your situation and the relationships that surround you can change the outcome toward your expected end. Let the reader beware, once you hear yourself saying something about change, you release a powerful dynamic designed by God dating back to Genesis. There is power in your words. The Bible says that God framed the world by His words (Heb. 11:3), and I believe we should do the same. Speak life over your situation and the relationships that surround you. I encourage my family to "change your confession" over your *Life Assignment*, because your words have an effect on what you expect to happen. Thinking one way and speaking another is hypercritical and self-defeating.

Change What You Do. It is commonly stated that it takes twenty-one days to break or establish a habit. I agree. I will add, however, that the first step toward doing something is the MOST important move you can make. If you are in a place of stagnation, if your career has seemingly plateaued, if your relationship has gotten stale... do something! One move can propel you and prepare you for your next Life Assignment in ways you couldn't imagine possible! Here's a simple tasker I have given to myself lately...*Do what you can't do, until you can, learn something you didn't know until you do!*

Change What You Think. The Bible says, *"as a man thinketh in his heart so is he"* (Prov. 23:7). When your thought Life aligns with what you say and what you do, you are on your way toward a better tomorrow. The idea of thinking back to previous missed opportunities can be depressing; however, in light of your next Life Assignment, your thoughts will cause you to have a different approach toward the next time a favorable opportunity or person comes your way!

Change Your Associations. When I asked my church members which of these approaches toward your next assignment was most important, they unanimously said changing your associations was at the top of the list. For some reason, their associations affected what they said, what they did, and what they thought. Amazing! I believe that it is possible to become a victim of your environment and the people who dwell in them. when you get to a point of change, you will look more closely at the people around. People who are negative, pessimistic, and defeatist are toxic to anyone desiring to embrace their next *Life Assignment* with passion and determination.

I believe God orchestrates people to come into your life and the right time to bless your life and help you prepare for your next season. That is exciting to me! I encourage the readers of this book to look carefully at the people surrounding you. Are they your Partners, who come along-side of you to add to your life, are they Pirates, who rob you of your dreams and ambitions, or are they Parasites, who only want to get what they can from you before they leave you hurt and alone?

UNDERSTANDING KAIROS

Kairos is an ancient Greek word meaning the right or opportune moment (the favorable moment). It signifies a time period, a moment of indeterminate time in which something special happens. I teach that there are: *Kairos Places* (Where I am assigned), *Kairos People* (Who I am assigned to) and *Kairos Opportunity* (What I am I assigned to do).

I teach that whenever someone encountered Jesus it was a *Kairos* moment; I even called Jesus, my *Kairos Man*. Let me give you an example. In Mark 5, we find the story of a woman who had an issue of blood,

"Now there was a woman who had been suffering from hemorrhages for twelve years. She had endured much under many physicians, and had spent all that she had; and she was no better, but rather grew worse. Then she had heard about Jesus, and came up behind him in the crowd and touched his cloak, for she said, *"If I but touch his clothes, I will be made well."* Mark 5:25-28.

Kairos...the right person at the right place, and at the right time. A favorable opportunity has appeared, and she took full advantage of it. She rudely pressed her way through the crowd; she raised her level of faith and touched the hem of Jesus' garment. The bottom line is that she received her healing THAT day!

Here's a true story... we had a faithful spiritual daughter in our church who was active duty in the military. She had a daughter who was borderline autistic and required specialized care. When her assignment came up to relocate, she was distraught because the gaining base did not have the medical facility to handle her daughter's condition. She called everyone she could think of to get her assignment canceled. She sent letters, prayed, cried, and did what any mother would do when faced with a desperate situation.

One day, a lady came in our church and fell in love with our ministry; she joined the church after her second time attending our services. During her New Members orientation, she shared how she had been recently assigned to the Air Force Base in our city as a relocation specialist-but it was only a temporary assignment. But while she was here, she wanted to grow spiritually, learn more about her Bible and get in a church where she could get a Word that was understandable and relevant. She also revealed that her job on the base was to help families with hardship relocation issues. We were floored!

Can you imagine the sense of awe in that room, like something divine was happening right before our eyes? Here was a person in the right job, at the right time, in the right place for the right purpose. It was a moment!

She expressed a confidence that reassured all of us that God was answering our prayers through this lady -who simply wanted to join a church where she could receive a word that would draw her closer to God.

She did what she always does. She helped our spiritual daughter get reassigned to a base where there is more than enough adequate medical facilities to take care of her daughter. Here's the kicker…after the reassignment, within two months the relocation specialist got an assignment in California to a base where a friend of mine is a local pastor.

On top of all of this, our spiritual daughter is praising God, was recently promoted and her daughter is doing well. Her testimony is *"Wont He do it?"*

It is situations like this that I believe are divinely orchestrated by God to bless your life!

YOUR PLACE CALLED "THERE"

---※---

When a person lands at their assigned place, I call it "There." "THERE" is not just a physical location; it is a place of <u>destiny and purpose</u>. Spiritually speaking, it is where you experience God's provision, purpose, plans, protection, promises, and the prophetic. Two examples.

In the first example, 1 Kings 17:2- *4-6 "...There I have commanded the ravens to feed thee "THERE". Here, the great prophet Elijah is told by the Lord to "Hide thyself" by the brook Cherith.

> "So he went and did according unto the word of the Lord: for he went and dwelt by the brook Cherith, that is before Jordan. And the ravens brought him bread and flesh in the morning, and bread and flesh in the evening; and he drank of the brook."

The interesting thing about this passage is that ravens are scavengers, they don't give to anyone–they take! But when you arrive at your place called *"There"*, God will reverse the natural order of the raven and command them to bring you provisions to fulfil your *Life Assignment*.

The second example comes from I Kings 17:9 "I have commanded a widow woman "THERE" to sustain thee". The story line is found in verses 10-16. It is a powerful passage that shows God will provide despite the circumstances. The audacity of Elijah to say to a poor widow,

"Make me a cake <u>first</u> and bring it to me, and afterward make one for you and your son."

Her *Kairos* moment was facilitated by her faith and obedience. She actually did what he said; *"... and she and he and her house did eat many days. And the barrel of meal wasted not neither did the cruse of oil fail – just as Elisha said."*

In the work place, changing jobs is not as important as progressing toward your place called "THERE". If God sends you "THERE" and you don't go for it, don't blame Him if you wind up, frustrated, disappointed, broke, and unfulfilled."

No one can fulfill that place of destiny for you; your next miracle depends on you getting t your pace called "There."

LIFE DURING YOUR "OFF SEASON"

Even though we have been talking about your seasons, I want to express a seemingly contrasting point to help the readers. What do you do between your last miracle and your next one? I try to keep track of the Jewish holidays and celebrations calendar. I believe they know something about Life Cycles that we Christians can learn a few things from. As I said earlier, God does not have to wait until September to declare the Autumn season has started. He simply changes the weather, and we all have to adjust. In San Angelo, it is not uncommon to see someone in flip-flops in December because thcy want to hold on to a season that is coming to an end.

What do you tell someone who has not made the adjustments, denied their *Kairos* assignment and seems to have missed their chance to transition. What do you tell a person who just got out of a lethargic relationship that wasn't going anywhere and still wants to be in a healthy, loving one? I say do what athletes do. Prepare yourself during the "Off-Season."

Right now, there are professional athletes preparing themselves for what will take place in their <u>next season</u>. The "off season" is that time in between where you are now and your next miracle or breakthrough. What you do during the off season, is CRITICAL because it prepares you for how successful you will be in the next.

Any athlete will tell you…it's what you do during the "off-season" that prepares you for your new season. Off season is…what you do in between jobs, career moves, ministry opportunities or relationships. I recently heard some athletes say, "*For me, there is no off-season;*" because there is constant preparation for what coming next in a persons' life

When I looked on-line to see the off- season workout routines for Usain Bolt, LeBron James, Jerry Rice, and Simone Biles, I was amazed to see how INSANE their workout routine was! But the reality is that even world class athletes don't wait until the season starts to get in shape; <u>their conditioning starts during the off season.</u>

During the off-season, they watch hours of film of themselves and their opponents. Right now, some rookie is studying the routes, habits, and plays of the veterans. They do strength drills, diet, exercise, yoga and more… just to give them the proper preparation to meet on the battlefield of their sport.

I used to tell my sons when they were younger, "While you're watching TV and playing video games, some kid across town is working on their skill-set to meet you on the court."

I submit to you that during the "off season" of our lives, we should press toward God, pray without ceasing, fast, study, serve, and give, with the passion and consistency of a world-class athlete. On a more practical note, I know we can't watch tape of ourselves, but we can review in our mind and heart, "What went wrong? Then improve on your own attitude, health, presentation and appearance and break bad habits.

Can I bless you with a scripture that I found truly amazing? Leviticus 25:5; "*And your threshing shall reach unto the vintage, and the vintage shall reach unto the sowing time: and ye shall eat your bread to the full, and dwell in your land safely.*"

> (MSG) *I will send the rains in their seasons, the ground will yield its crops and the trees of the field their fruit. You will thresh until the grape harvest and the grape harvest will continue until planting time; you'll have more than enough to eat and will live safe and secure in your land.*

Spiritually speaking...

Before <u>David</u> became king of Israel, during his off-season he was a shepherd.

Before <u>Moses</u> became the great deliverer, during his off-season, he herded cattle.

Before <u>Paul</u> became the great apostle, during his off-season he was a Pharisee.

Before <u>Jesus</u> revealed himself as our Lord and Savior, he was found in the temple as a youngster, asking questions and dialoging with the priests and rabbis.

I told my church to "fill in the blank", Before I became a _____ , I <u>Whatever you are doing now</u>!

ONE MORE STORY FROM THE BEVERLY HILLBILLIES

This is a conversation took place between Jed and his cousin Pearl while Jed was contemplating moving to California. Unbelievable!

> Jed Clampett: *What do you think Pearl? You think I oughta move?*

> Cousin Pearl Bodine: *Jed, how can you even ask? Look around you. You live eight miles from your nearest neighbor. You're overrun with skunks, possums, coyotes, and bobcats. You use kerosene lamps for light. You cook on a wood stove, summer and winter. You're drinkin' homemade moonshine, and washin' with home-made lye soap. And your bathroom is fifty feet from the house. And you ask should you move ?*

> Jed Clampett: [ponders all this] *Yeah, I reckon you're right. Man'd be a dang fool to leave all this.*

WORDS WE LIVE BY

When a person lands at their assigned place, I call it "There". "THERE" is not just a physical location; it is a place of <u>destiny and purpose</u> The Bible is a book about relationships

When you arrive at your place called 'There," God will reverse the natural order of the raven and command them to bring you provisions to fulfil your life assignment

In the workplace, changing jobs is not as important as progressing toward your place called "THERE". If God's sends you "THERE" and you don't go for it, don't blame Him if you wind up, frustrated, disappointed, broke, and unfulfilled

Right now, there are professional athletes preparing themselves for what will take place in the next season. The "off season" is that time in between where you are now and your next miracle or breakthrough. What you do during the off season, is CRITICAL, it prepares you for how successful you will be in the next

I submit to you that during the "off season" of our lives, we should press toward God, pray without ceasing, fast, study, serve and give, with the passion and consistency of a world-class athlete.

EYES HAVENT SEEN

I Corinthian 2:7, 8, 9,10

> (MSG) *God's wisdom is something myste-*
> *rious that goes deep into the interior of his pur-*
> *poses. You don't find it lying around on the*
> *surface. It's not the latest message, but more*
> *like the oldest — what God determined as the*
> *way to bring out his best in us, long before we*
> *ever arrived on the scene. The experts of our*
> *day haven't a clue about what this eternal plan*
> *is. If they had, they wouldn't have killed the*
> *Master of the God-designed life on a cross. As*
> *it is written:*
>
> *No one's ever seen or heard anything like this,*
> *Never so much as imagined anything quite*
> *like it — What God has arranged for those*
> *who love him.*

Verse 10 says, *"But you've seen and heard it because God by his Spirit has brought it all out into the open before you"* *"As it is written"*, means that Paul is quoting a verse that was spoken before. The time he is referencing is Isaiah 64:4 where the children of Israel are looking for some indication that God is with them, so they...

1. Petitioned that God would appear wonderfully for them.
2. Desired that God would vanquish all opposition toward them.
3. Desired that His actions would bring such glory and honor of God, that the name of Jehovah would be clearly known, not only to their friends, but to His adversaries likewise, that they may know it and tremble at his presence.

Much of it was concealed in former ages, but they knew it not, because the unsearchable riches of Christ were hidden in God, they were hidden from the wise and prudent, but in these latter days they were revealed by the gospel, so the apostle applies this (1 Cor. 2:9), for it follows (v. 10), but God has revealed them unto us by His Spirit; that which men had not heard since the beginning of the world they should hear before the end of it, and at the end of it should see, when the veil shall be rent to introduce the glory that is yet to be revealed. God himself knew what He had in store for believers, but none knew besides Him.

No one can comprehend it but God himself, because His understanding is infinite.

I understand the part that says, "*Eye hath not seen*", I even understand the part that says, *"Ear has not heard"*, however, it is this next part that continues to challenge my faith; *"neither has it entered into the heart of man, the things which God has prepared for them that love Hhim."*

This part tells me that there are things God has stored up for me that has not even entered into my heart yet! ITS PROPHETIC! I can't even believe for them because God has not revealed them to me yet...nevertheless, they exist, they are stored up, prepared for me... simply because ... HE LOVES ME!

In terms of SEASONS, we know that God is not limited to our days, months, and years. Because He is the Alpha & Omega, the beginning and the end, the One who WAS and IS and IS TO COME... His presence is already existent in seasons that we haven't experienced yet. Consider these scriptures...

> Romans 4:17 *As it is written, I have made thee (Abraham) a father of many nations,) before him whom he believed, even God, who quickeneth the dead, and calleth those things which be not as though they were.*

> Ecclesiastes 3:9-15 *He hath made everything beautiful in his time: also he hath set the world in their heart, so that no man can find out the work that God maketh from the beginning to the end. I know that, whatsoever God doeth, it shall be forever: nothing can be put to it, nor any thing taken from it: and God doeth it, that men should fear before him. That which hath been, is now; and that which is to be, hath already been; and God requireth that which is past.*

Only God can do this! This radically changed my life, my family, and my ministry. Because I cannot see into tomorrow, let alone into the next season for my family, my church, or myself, I have to embrace that God will send the right <u>people</u> at the right <u>time</u> with the right <u>resources</u> to bless my life!

My hope is that the God who holds my future will continue to unfold and reveal His blessings to me and my family. The idea that He has blessings, challenges, opportunities, and encounters that I have yet to experience–yet, in His domain, they already exist.

I hope that the readers of this book will look carefully at their lives in light of Divine Relationships. Indeed, they are orchestrated by God to bless your life!

WORDS WE LIVE BY

- Much of it was concealed in former ages; they knew it not, because the unsearchable riches of Christ were hidden in God he Bible is a book about relationships.

- There are things God has stored up for me that has not even entered into my heart yet! ITS PROPHETIC!

- The Father has a need that only we (as His children) can fulfill. In all of His omnipotence, His omnipresence, and His omniscience, He has a need, and that need is to have His children reconciled to Him.

- In terms of SEASONS, we know that God is not limited to our days, months and years. Because He is the Alpha and Omega, the beginning and the end, the One who WAS and IS and IS TO COME… His presence is already existent in seasons that we haven't experienced yet.

- I have to embrace that God will send the <u>right people</u> at the <u>right time</u> with the <u>right resources</u> to bless my life!
- My hope is that the God who holds my future will continue to unfold and reveal his blessings to me and my family. The idea that He has blessings, challenges, opportunities, and encounters that I have yet to experience–yet, in His domain, they already exist.

PRAYER FOR THE READERS

Father, in the name of Jesus, I lift up the readers of this book before you. I pray that the eyes of their understanding will be opened to the divine truths You have declared in Your Word long before we were ever born.

I pray that the Author and Finisher of Life will surround you will people and favorable opportunities to bless your life.

I pray the Genesis Principles found in this book will bring revelation to their understanding and when they read and re-read this book, they will discover that you have created processes to lead them to a life in Christ Jesus and that more abundantly.

I come against any and all toxic relationships in their lives and they will be drawn to healthy people, healthy places, and healthy opportunities.

Lastly, I pray that they will apply whatever insights this book has provided to their family, their church, or the business and you will prove your Word works, when we work the Word!

CPSIA information can be obtained
at www.ICGtesting.com
Printed in the USA
LVHW012024070620
657583LV00006B/964